OF THEE I *Sing*

A Musical Journey of Faith

DIANNE COON

WESTBOW·
PRESS
A DIVISION OF THOMAS NELSON
& ZONDERVAN

WestBow Press books may be ordered through booksellers or by contacting:

WestBow Press
A Division of Thomas Nelson & Zondervan
1663 Liberty Drive
Bloomington, IN 47403
www.westbowpress.com
1 (866) 928-1240

ISBN: 978-1-4908-2388-1 (sc)
ISBN: 978-1-4908-2391-1 (hc)
ISBN: 978-1-4908-2389-8 (e)

Library of Congress Control Number: 2014901561

Printed in the United States of America.

WestBow Press rev. date: 2/25/2014

Contents

The song began and the angels danced
As the rain fell to the earth,
Quenching the thirst of beautiful flowers
Everywhere.

"The stones will cry out!"
Luke 19:40

Introduction

Music has been a constant companion throughout my life, starting as a child learning to play the piano and continuing as an adult participating in high school, college, and church choirs. It was not until I became a member of a Christian church in California that I realized how music fills not only the heart of the listener but also the performer. The beautiful words of the hymns I learned allowed me to show my love for God by singing a prayer. It became my way to worship.

Twenty years ago, I formed a singing group called Spice of Life and entertained nursing-home and retirement-home residents in the central California area. The music we sang filled our hearts with blessings as we shared with people unable to attend church. I thought of our visits as the last watering hole for those at the end of their lives. If I could give them a taste of the living water by sharing many old hymns telling of Jesus and His love for all, perhaps their lives would not end with despair.

I've learned to depend on God in times of trouble and strife and have included in this book many of my life lessons. It is *Of Thee I Sing*.

SECTION 1

Getting Ready

CHAPTER 1

Fitting the Octave

I love music, and I especially love a piano. It's a mystery to me how each piano can have its own sound and character, whether old or new, in tune or not. I've never been able to walk by one without pushing a key or two, just to hear its voice. I remember the first time I saw a piano. It was love at first sight. "In love with a piano?" you say. It's true. The love affair has lasted a lifetime.

You might imagine that the first piano I saw was a beautiful, black, baby grand accompanied by a bench supporting a red velvet cushion. You might imagine it was positioned in the center of a grand music store, sparkling and reflecting the overhead lights. You might even imagine it was the envy of all who entered that music store. It was not.

Actually, the first piano I saw was wrapped with yellow straps and was being pushed and pulled up two flights of stairs by six men with a lot of rope. Finally, it was pushed across the floor and came to rest safely in the center of my grandparents' parlor. We all just stood silently and stared, including Mom and Dad, my sister, my brother, Grandma, Uncle Louie, Uncle Steve, and two neighbors, as the men were catching their breaths while wiping their sweaty necks. Mom started to ask about the bench just as my grandpa pushed his way through the spectators with a stool held high in the air. I remember that stool. It was walnut, just like the piano. It had twisted legs with glass-ball claw feet. Grandpa plopped it down in front of the piano, twirled the top to just the right height, and sat down. He looked up at us, grinned, and stated out of the side of his mouth, "Let's see if the old girl held her pitch."

He threw open the dustcover, positioned his boney fingers over the keys, and began to play a waltz. His music filled the huge empty parlor as he tapped his foot and smiled from ear to ear. The piano never sounded better.

It was over sixty years ago that I stood in that parlor and listened to music that would influence my whole life. Our family moved into the redbrick and gray-clapboard mansion on Franklin Street in Auburn, New York. The house had four stories, including the basement and an attic. It was in that attic that my dad found the trunk full of old music—music that my grandma could play effortlessly. It was old sheet music that I've since given to my daughter. The basement was divided into four rooms: one for coal, one for canned goods, one for storage, and the last for my brother's model train. The first and second floors each had eight rooms. There were two sets of stairs: one in the back and one in the front. This was a very big house.

Three families lived in that big old mansion: my mom, dad, sister, brother, and I on the first floor and my grandparents on the second floor. After my dad finished creating a two-room apartment, my great-aunt joined the upstairs residents. This was, by the way, the third house, where my grandparents lived upstairs with their piano. My poor dad—three times he had to get that huge musical instrument up at least one flight of stairs, and this time two. It was definitely a labor of love, because both my grandparents and my father played the piano.

I remember watching my grandparents as each played that old brown upright. Grandpa was a tall man with a ring of white hair circling his head just above his ears. He wore bright-blue suspenders that stretched to hold up his black-striped pants. He leaned his cane against the side of the piano until it eventually crashed to the floor as his nimble fingers played ragtime music that rattled all the dishes in Grandma's buffet. He couldn't read a note. In contrast, Grandma played church music, reading lines of tiny black dots written on large sheets of yellow paper. She was a slight woman standing taller than she measured with one long, gray braid held back from her face by brown combs that she constantly adjusted. Her name was Laura, but my grandfather called her Mother. His name was Louis, but she called him Daddy. I didn't know my grandparents well, but I do remember their music.

My dad played that same piano, and he, like his dad, couldn't read music. Times were tough during his childhood in the twenties and thirties, and lessons were out of the question. But I think the music was in him because he learned to play by ear, mostly on the black keys. What I mean by playing by ear is that he could listen to a tune and duplicate it on the piano. He combined the sounds that his mother made, which were all flats and sharps using the black keys, and the style of ragtime that his father played. My dad's music still resonates in my head as I remember the old polkas, waltzes, and popular ballads he played.

I was nine years old and just starting summer vacation when my dad and mom decided we would move to the country. Grandma and Grandpa were not coming with us this time, at least not right away. They went to stay with my aunt in Batavia while my dad got their apartment ready in the new house. I don't remember packing up my stuff; I suppose I was too young. I do remember saying good-bye to my best friend, Marsha. It was one of many sad good-byes I have collected throughout my life.

The ride to the country lasted a long time and was uneventful, until we turned onto Cooper Street, a dirt road. No one could ever explain to me why a dirt road would be called a street. As we traveled down the road, the car filled up with dust, causing us to cough and lose our breaths. Finally, we pulled into the driveway, quickly opened the doors, and piled out so we could breathe. We all stood around took deep breaths, feeling very glad to be at our destination.

The house stood all by itself and was surrounded by weeds. It looked dead to me. *Is this where we were going to live?* I thought. I always wonder about the memories we store and the ones we dismiss. I don't remember unpacking anything or seeing piles of furniture that needed to be placed efficiently throughout the house. What I do remember is that there were no sidewalks. I had the sinking feeling that I would never be able to roller-skate again. I knew that I would have to throw away my chalk; hopscotch was out of the question. The house was horrible! It was old with no running water, no furnace for heat, and no bathroom. I realized that living in the country was not going to be easy.

The piano came to the country with us, and instead of being hoisted up flights of stairs, the brown upright was placed on the first floor in the part of the house where my grandparents were going to live. After my grandparents moved in, my dad would visit his mom and play the piano. I often sat next to him while he played his waltzes and polkas. I would hear the music, stop whatever I was doing outside, and race to Grandma's living room. I grabbed the old dining-room chair and scraped it across the worn linoleum floor until I was right next to the twirly-topped stool where my dad sat. His arm would brush against my shoulder as his fingers flew over the keys. I was always amazed and so wished I could do the same. When I tried, there was only noise. I constantly asked my dad how I could learn to play with more than one finger. I wanted to stretch my hand and play an octave using my thumb and little finger, but my hands were too small! Perhaps you're wondering about this word *octave*. An octave is the interval of eight degrees between two musical tones, or eight white piano keys. It was a pretty difficult stretch for a nine-year-old. I wasn't ready to just sit and play. Dad would chuckle and tell me not to worry. Soon enough, my hands would grow.

I realized throughout my growing years that there were many octaves I had to grow into. I was an impatient child, always wanting something just out of reach. I wanted to be older and taller. I wanted curly hair, not straight. I was not content just being me. I constantly looked to the future instead of enjoying the present. I made many mistakes because I was too eager to be something I was not prepared to be. I was selfish in my wants and thought of only myself.

It took a couple of years for me to reach that octave on the piano, but it has taken me a lifetime to learn to be happy in present situations. I finally realized that being patient while learning and practicing allowed me to reach any destination with ease. Most importantly, it allowed me to be prepared. As I matured, I grew in mind, body, and spirit. I learned to trust in God to supply my way.

Today, I'm in my sixties, but how I wish to be nine again, to sit next to my dad and watch his fingers fly over the keys as he played those old waltzes and polkas. If I sit real still on my piano bench and close my eyes, I can almost feel his arm brushing against my shoulder.

My song of praise: "In My Life, Lord, Be Glorified" by unknown.
Bible quote: (Ecclesiastes 3:1 NAS) "There is an appointed time for everything. And there is a time for every event under heaven."

My Dad

CHAPTER 2

Start on the Right Note

A musical note is a sound of definite pitch and a symbol denoting its duration. A key on a piano or an instrument plays a note, and a vocalist sings a note. The first note of any composition is important. It seems uncommon that any of us would worry about the first note of a song, unless that first note is wrong. Music can be comforting to the ear as a song sung or played on an instrument. If, in starting a song, that first note is wrong, the whole song will crash and burn. When performing music vocally, finding the beginning note can be a challenge. How do we know what the first note is? If we have a piano, we can look at sheet music and follow the directions, or we can purchase a CD and listen and practice. Many songs that I have learned over the years have taken weeks of practice.

Life is a little different. We aren't born with a manufacturer's guidebook. My parents did a certain amount of teaching and guiding, but only for twenty-odd years. After that, I was pretty much on my own. We can't listen and practice our lives until we get it right. I actually looked for some kind of guidebook when I received the gift basket from the hospital after my first child was born. There was no book. My mom helped, but I learned by experience. Just to make life a little more interesting, each child I had after the first was entirely different, and still there was no book.

Starting out in life is similar to singing. Finding that first note can be challenging and the hardest beginning to anything we attempt. It can be a word or action, a decision or a lack of one, a plan, or a choice made. There are many outside influences affecting our start. Family members, friends, and teachers seem to be waiting on the sidelines to influence our decisions and choices. I think everything done in life has a first note.

My first life experience didn't necessarily start on the right note, but it was the only one I knew at the time. When I was eighteen, I created and stored a plan for my life in my mind and heart. As a young woman finishing high school, it became very important to me that I find a husband, lest I become a spinster at the age of twenty. Can you imagine? There is so much I could have done, but the influence of society tainted my decision-making process. My parents thought I wasn't smart enough to attend college, even though I had a B+ average. If the truth is known, it wasn't my aptitude that was in question but the cost. Therefore, I decided that marriage was the only way out of the house and into the world. All my classmates were headed down the church aisle. Why not me?

My song began, and the first note was a young man who professed his love to me. I was young and wanted to be loved. I didn't do what I should have done, and what I did was wrong. I should have gone to college. I did not. I wanted to be like all the other girls in my high-school senior class: to get married and have children. I wanted to have my own home. After all, I was eighteen. Isn't that old enough to take on all those tremendous responsibilities?

My plan moved right along. We were married in a small village church, vowing to love one another until death. We both worked. I was a legal secretary, and he was a carpenter's apprentice. It's funny how you get lulled into a false sense of security as time passes. My firstborn was a daughter. Four years later, a son was born, and four years after that, another son came along. We bought a house, fixed it up, and sold it. We bought his father's farm and attempted to be farmers. We worked, raised children, and played.

When did my song crash and burn? While I wasn't looking.

You may ask, "Did you start on the right note? Was it the right note for you?" I really thought it was. Only in retrospect do I realize that my choices were based on what everyone else was doing. I followed the crowd. Impatience was my constant companion as I worked to change my husband to what I thought he should be. I didn't consider his first note. I know he must have had one, but I didn't slow down long enough to listen to his song. We all know where that action can lead. Failure! We both made mistakes that we just didn't know how to correct. My plan hadn't worked, and everything got out of order in my mind. I couldn't remember the melody to my song, so the first note seemed forever lost. I realized that I would have to find a new note to start a new plan.

We don't always see ahead with clarity. Sometimes, the implications of our choices are hard to anticipate, and sometimes we think only in the moment. There were many songs I sang: marriage, childbirth, divorce, second marriage, the death of my parents, different jobs, and moving more than twenty times. I started many of my songs on the wrong note, but I was never afraid to stop the music and start again.

The proper order of life is sometimes elusive, and we're often not patient in waiting and preparing for life's journey. Looking into the future can feel like you're lost in fog. After almost a whole lifetime, I found answers in the Bible to my many questions. My life changed when I joined a church and began to sing in a choir. The words to the many songs I learned ministered to my confusion and eventually lifted my personal fog.

Music is present throughout the Bible, from Genesis to Revelation. God entreats musicians throughout the ages to use their melodies to draw people closer to worship and ignite spiritual passion in times of war and peace. Music is the lotion that soothes the rawness of life. Simple songs and complex songs, easy and difficult instrumentals, melodies and harmonies, fast rhythms and slow, high and low notes—all fill the listeners with joy and healing. Everyone participates. Everyone starts on the first note. I thank God for beautiful music that has mended my heart many times. I thank God for the songs I have been able to sing back to Him in worship.

I learned that starting on the right note is important, but if that note sours the beginning, total failure is not necessarily eminent. The promises of God shine through, giving us comfort and confidence. Jeremiah's words from God to his children of yesterday show us that God doesn't change; He is the same today.

My song of praise: "Standing on the Promises of God" by R. Kelso Carter. Bible quote: (Jeremiah 29:11–13 NAS) "'For I know the plans that I have for you,' declares the Lord, 'plans for welfare and not calamity to give you a future and a hope. Then you will call upon Me and come and pray to Me, and I will listen to you. And you will seek Me and find Me when you search for Me with all your heart.'"

CHAPTER 3

Keep the Melody True

A melody is a linear succession of musical tones, which is perceived as a single entity. Every song has a melody, even though sometimes it can be hidden or convoluted. Most often, the structure of a song starts with the verse and is followed by the prechorus or chorus. It's within the chorus that the main melody is heard. This is the section that listeners will be able to repeat after hearing it several times. This is where the lyrics are exciting, telling the main idea of the song.

I have heard music on the radio that sounded familiar, a song that was somewhat like I remembered but just a little different. Sometimes, the vocalist moves the musical notes around in a way that hides the original melody in an effort to make it their own, thereby almost changing the song. Whatever the case, the melody is no longer true to its inception.

My mother loved music, especially the songs from the 1940s and 1950s when the popular singers sang with straight melodies. Every morning, as we ate breakfast and waited for the school bus, she had the radio playing. She always remarked how much she loved the songs and how they were sung. She would tell us, "Now this song is being sung correctly, not like some of those singers who mess up a good song by making up their own melodies. Sometimes, you can't even understand the words or the melody." She would always get seriously worked up about it. The men who sang those songs were traditionalists and very popular, obviously her favorite crooners. Mom often told me of the times as a teenage girl in the 1940s when she would go to the amusement park in the city where she lived so she could listen to the music of the big bands. Harry James, Benny Goodman, and the Dorsey Brothers would stop over at the pavilion in Auburn, New York, while on tour. She knew all their music and would sometimes get up and sing with the band.

Music was all around me as I grew up. To this day, I am most comfortable when I recognize a song's melody true to the way it was written. My personality is one of balance, rules of order, and correctness. I embrace the familiar and struggle with change. My mother's parents were police officers. In fact, all the relatives on her side were involved with some kind of law and order. I was raised in a legalistic home with mom as the alpha ruler, and she ruled with an iron fist. It was a "No, you can't" attitude as I grew up. Therefore, I tried everything. I knew what I wanted and wouldn't take no for an answer, at least not without causing confusion and mayhem. My mother called me "a willful child." In retrospect, I realize that I truly was willful.

I was a middle child with an older brother who was the apple of my mother's eye and a younger sister who could do no wrong. My brother was five years my senior and had no time for me. The fact is he probably hated that I wanted to be around him all the time. Even so, I loved and idolized him, at least until he left for the National Guard. When he came back, he married his high-school sweetheart, and that was pretty much the last I saw of him. My sister was three years younger than I was and was attached to my side most of the time. I loved my sister, but I didn't have patience for her. It would seem that I treated her much like my brother treated me. This was something I would later regret.

We grew up together in the country on a dirt road with no sidewalks. There were many fun times and many remarkable memories—some good and some not so good.

My sister was sweet, quiet, and always pleasant. I was not. She had strawberry-blonde, naturally curly hair, blue eyes, and a complexion like peaches and cream. I had straight, black hair and green eyes that could throw a glare stronger than the sun filtering through a dirty window. I also had freckles, which I hated. My mother would always point out to everyone in our family how my sister had these tiny little curls that glistened with perspiration and stuck to her forehead during humid July afternoons. With me, it was different. She would pull my long, straight, black hair into two tightly twisted braids while complaining about the project as my eyes slanted with tears that threatened to escape. Everyone loved my sister and basically ignored me.

I have always laughingly referred to my sister as Snow White. On the other hand, I likened myself to Rose Red. You might be saying to yourself, "Who on earth was Rose Red?" Let me offer an explanation. When I was younger, on TV there was a cartoon show called *Rocky the Flying Squirrel*, which was created by Jay Ward and Alex Anderson. On that show, they featured a segment called fractured fairy tales. One of the fairy tales they fractured was *Snow White and the Seven Dwarfs,* written by Jacob Grimm and Wilhelm Grimm. Rose Red was the star and an exact opposite of Snow White. She was wicked and a troublemaker causing a great deal of trouble for Snow White. Unfortunately, that seemed to fit the scenario of my childhood with my sister.

The old house where my sister and I grew up was surrounded by fifty acres of land. I loved running through the fields, climbing the apple trees in an old, retired orchard, and tromping through the hedgerows that separated long-forgotten bean fields. I liked playing

Because I wasn't content with myself, I spent many years trying to change. I didn't realize that I had an inner melody. I later found out that it was a beautiful song. During my growing years, I compared what I was to what I saw in somebody else and found I could never quite measure up. I never felt good enough, pretty enough, nice enough, or actually *anything* enough. I was intent on changing myself. While attending high school, during summer vacations I'd put a plan together to be different come September. I'd tell myself that this would be the year I would not make any errors, I would not say anything hurtful, and I would not get into trouble. I tried so hard each year, only to fail.

I carried these wishes well into my adult years, until several years ago during a stroll at lunchtime with my friend and coworker from China. She was a very kind, loving person who cared about me. We shared our lives with each other, our accomplishments, and our failures. I told her of my inability to like the way I was. I complained about everything from my weight to my lack of patience. One day as we were walking and I was complaining, she stopped, turned around, and placed her hand on my arm. She then told me that I should be happy with the way I was. She said, "Because if you were different, you wouldn't be Dianne and no one would recognize you."

Keeping a melody true in music allows the listeners to recognize the song. Just as in human nature, it's important to understand yourself and stay genuine to what you are so that you will be recognized. Music and the love of a song soothed my rough edges and gave me comfort. I think we all carry a song in our hearts. It's our personal melody that defines us. We may be born with it or learn it throughout life's journey. It could be a simple melody or a complicated string of notes; nonetheless, it is pure and lovely to observe. We hear it when we compliment someone who has tried so hard to please us. We hear it when we express thanks to a tired servant. We hear it when we say, "I love you," to our spouse or that special friend. We hear it when we smile at a stranger.

The song in my heart has been the same for over forty years. I know it's there because I hear it when I am very quiet. When I wake in the morning, it's there. When I lie down for the evening and drift to sleep, it's there. My song is a melody of praise and love to my God. It starts with "Dear God, of Thee I sing." My true melody is that inner voice that keeps me at peace.

I have learned that I cannot change what I am. All that I have seen and touched, all that I have learned and experienced, dwells within me. It's okay if I don't fit in. I don't need to be like everyone else. I will continue to enhance my good qualities and repair those rough edges. I will keep my melody true, my song that defines me. I just have to remember to listen. Because whatever my situation in life has been or may be, it seems that once a melody is set, it changes not.

My song of praise: "He Is Able" by Greg Ferguson.
Bible quote: (Philippians 4:8–9 NAS) "Finally, brethren, whatever is true, whatever is honorable, whatever is right, whatever is pure, whatever is lovely, whatever is of good repute, if there is any excellence and if anything worthy of praise, let your mind dwell on these things."

SECTION 2

Dealing with Life

CHAPTER 4

The Do-Re-Mis of Life

In music, there's the term *solfeggio*. It's an instructive technique for the teaching of sight-singing, in which each note of the score is sung to a special syllable called a "solfege syllable." The seven syllables commonly used for this practice in English-speaking countries are "do-re-mi-fa-so-la-ti-do." Does that sound familiar? While attending elementary school, children are taught to sing this musical scale. Most of us at some point in our lives have heard the song that starts with "Doe, a deer, a female deer." It's from the movie *The Sound of Music* by Richard Rodgers and Oscar Hammerstein.

"Do-re-mi" (or C, D, and E in musical notation) are the first three notes of the musical scale and can be compared to three distinct personalities. We are all as different as those first three notes. The first and base note is "do." The dissonant note, or the very next sound, is "re." The third in line is "mi," which is considered the harmony note. A person's way of behaving can replicate these three categories.

Consider "do," the first sound. A person who represents "do" is most often the first at everything. They are the steady beginner starting the song, a sentence, an action, or nothing at all. A "do" person can always be counted on to be there with strong conviction and sound. "Let's start at the very beginning …" Or so the song goes.

The second sound is "re." A person who represents "re" can sometimes be contrary or argumentative. The sound that grates or causes discomfort to our ears is the very next note on the musical scale. Even if that person makes us feel uncomfortable, dissonance is needed. It is that need that causes questions and makes for answers to be brought forth. "Re" gives us variety and interest.

The third sound is "mi." A person who represents "mi" is the third in line and sometimes will take the harmony in music. The "mi" person is the diplomat, the arbitrator, the one who sees both sides of the trio, and can be the blend in life.

Without the harmony or the dissonant sound, what would "do" accomplish? There would always be just a single sound of music, one side of an argument or no argument at all, just complacency. We would tire of that quickly.

Early in my life, I most represented a "do." I was always first in line and ready to take over without a thought as to how anyone else felt. I was never a "re." I saw more than enough dissonance as a child growing up. Confrontation was not comfortable for me. Being first and in control protected me, but I so wanted to be the "mi" note, the kind, easygoing, gentle follower. For years, I tried to make myself into that harmonizer. I knew that I needed to back off once in a while and learn how to blend with people.

As a young woman moving to the west coast from New York with a new husband, I had to learn about life all over again. I found many differences in state laws, rules, and people's attitudes. The first year in California was very difficult. I had left my pregnant daughter and her husband to move three thousand miles away. I also left my oldest son with his father, my ex-husband. I was headed for a new life with my second husband and my youngest son. I didn't realize what I was giving up to have this second chance at life. To this day, I can close my eyes and see my daughter standing in our old driveway in New York while waving good-bye as we headed up Route 38 to the New York State Thruway and on to California. For many years, that picture in my mind would bring me to tears.

For the first year after arriving in California, I was terribly homesick and missing all that I had known. I had secured a job as a purchasing agent for a small manufacturing company, only to practically come to blows with the office manager who feared for her position against such a smart college graduate as me. Try as I could, I could not make friends with that woman. I left after eight months and suffered a mild nervous breakdown. I had not come to grips with all that had changed in my life. Therefore, the change gripped me in an emotional sickness. Too much had changed in too short a period of time. I decided to stay home and put myself back together.

My husband and I attended a church that ministered to my many questions regarding the Bible. The Sunday services began a healing in my soul, and I began to feel whole once again. I loved the pastor and his teachings, the music was fantastic and uplifting, and we felt at home with the many friends we had made. After a year, I felt confident enough to think about working again. My church advertised for a computer operator position and I decided to submit my resume. I thought it would be the perfect place to work, a place where God was the main focus. I wasn't foolish enough to think the people would be perfect. I knew better. I did, however, think they would be different from the ordinary workplace. I was to find out they were not.

My conception of people was that they all thought the way I thought. Imagine my surprise when I came up against someone who was different. Many arguments ensued, and hard feelings prevailed. I was still the smarter-than-average New York college graduate. I was the steamroller that squashed people and their thoughts. I would look back, and they would be pasted to the floor. I would always wonder what was wrong with them. Why did they not think exactly as I did? I didn't realize how bad I'd become. I didn't realize that I was the problem.

I worked for the minister of finance as a computer operator in charge of teaching and offering support to the clerical staff of over fifteen. I loved my job. I loved working at the church. When I think back on that time, I remember that I felt like I was working for famous people: ministers who knew God! My husband and I were involved in several ministries, including the choir and the singles group. I felt like I was exactly in the right job. God had given me this wonderful position. Imagine my surprise when I arrived at the financial office to receive my yearly evaluation and found out that no one thought I was the grand person I perceived myself to be.

It was at the end of the day on Friday when my boss called me to his office. I was confident that I had done a wonderful job and just knew that I would receive an increase in pay. I sat down on the chair across from his desk, ready to hear glowing reports, folded my hands in my lap, and looked up. His face was not the face of a happy man. With his jaw set and his eyes staring at the pen he held between his thumb and index finger, he proceeded to tell me that something had to change. That familiar argument in me whispered, "Why did *I* have to change? Why can't they think like I think?" I was forty-three years old and felt like fifteen.

My boss went on to explain that I was insulting the other secretaries, hurting their feelings, and causing them to feel inadequate. I was bossy, arrogant, blunt, and rude. The attitude I portrayed was that I knew it all and they knew nothing. If I was going to keep my job, I needed to learn to get along with others. I would not receive a raise this year, until

I proved I was worthy. That is, until I proved that I was striving to learn how to get along with others.

I was truly a "do." It was the one personality trait I didn't want to be. I was the controller, the important one, and the first in line. I was miserable. *Great,* I thought, *I have once again proven my inability to get along in this world with other human beings.* I was devastated. I went back to my office, shut the computer down, and headed for the back door and the parking lot. I was barely able to keep the tears in my eyes.

I barged through the church doors and into the blaring sunlight, practically knocking over my friend Jim. He held my arm and asked what was wrong. I couldn't hold back the tears any longer and absolutely fell apart. I explained to him what had just happened at my yearly evaluation, and I think I also told him my life's story. I'm not sure. I only know that he was very instrumental in my growth as a person and a Christian.

Jim was the epitome of smooth. I would observe his interaction with the people he disagreed with and see the smile on his face and the gentle way he brought them to his way of thinking. They disagreed with him and loved him at the same time. He was truly a "mi." Why was I not like that? After getting in trouble with my boss because of my mouth and opinions, and after spilling my guts to Jim in the parking lot, I asked him how I could ever change to something I was not. I asked him how he was able to be so smooth and agreeable.

First, he told me that I would have to come to the conclusion that I wanted to change. He went on to explain that he had gone through the same life-changing situation. He gave the credit to Dale Carnegie and the class titled "Principles of Human Behavior." He asked if I would be interested in taking the course. It was very expensive, but he added that he had one more scholarship left and would give it to me if I was interested. I told him I would think about it.

On the drive home, I reflected on two things that had been said to me throughout my life. First, my mother always told me that I needed to read the book *How to Win Friends & Influence People,* oddly enough written by Carnegie. Most of the time, I took offense to her remarks. She had many! Of course, as I grew up, I didn't think anything was wrong with me. Secondly, my husband had also mentioned the book's title and the author. My friend had mentioned that name. I knew that there was a connection, and my husband had the answers.

Later that evening, I reviewed my horrible day with my husband. He, like my choir friend Jim, had taken the Dale Carnegie course many years ago. He admitted that he had learned a great deal and encouraged me to take the offer of a scholarship. It would seem I had no choice in the matter. I needed my job, and it looked like I needed overhauling. I had a lot of reservations, but I was not one to back down from a challenge. That Sunday after church, I talked to Jim and told him I would be interested in taking the class.

That twenty-week class changed my life. It did not change the way I was made, only the way I interacted with people. I have used the theories of that class for the last twenty-five years. I understand why people are different; they have to be. It's the mix that makes life interesting. It's the same mix that makes a choir sound so wonderful as it presents music. It's the "do-re-mi's."

Life has not been perfect for me and I still stumble every once in a while, but I know how to adjust. I understand myself better, thereby understanding others as well. There are thousands of books that teach us how to understand the differences in personalities and how to get along with others. The Bible tells story after story of human difficulties. I am not afraid to mix the voices and accept the differences in people because none of us are the same. We are all different with ideas of our own and an individual presence—as different as the first three notes of a music scale.

My song of praise: "Change My Heart, Oh God" by Eddie Espinosa. Bible quote: (Romans 14:19 NAS) "So let us pursue the things which make for peace and the building up of one another."

CHAPTER 5

Tweeters and Woofers

I first heard the words *tweeter* and *woofer* from my husband as he was setting up his newly purchased stereo system. I looked up the meanings in a couple of technical magazines. A tweeter is a loudspeaker designed to produce high audio frequencies, typically from around 2,000 Hz to 20,000 Hz (generally considered the upper limit of human hearing). Some tweeters can manage response up to 65 kHz. The name is derived from the high-pitched sounds made by some birds, especially in contrast to the low woofs made by many dogs after which low-frequency drivers are named woofers.

Electronics has never been a favorite subject of mine, mostly because I don't understand much more than the basics. I was happy if I could get a clear station on my radio. So you can understand my chagrin when my husband arrived home one evening with a pickup load of Radio Shack electronics. As he unloaded the pickup, he named each piece for me. There was a component system, including many parts and wires, a tape deck, a record player, a radio, an amplifier, two huge speakers, two small speakers, and four books with all kinds of schematics and directions. It was a mystery to me how he ever got it together, but he did.

The equalizer was the most interesting component with its six levers for each large speaker that had to be dialed in exactly for perfect sound. After everything was hooked up, and the speakers were placed strategically in the corners of our living room, we prepared ourselves for wonderful entertainment. My husband's first choice of music was a country-western tape by the group Alabama. The sound was stunning. I'm sure it was because we had tweeters and woofers. "Sit down!" my husband yelled over the sound of strumming guitars. "You're gonna love this." And, of course, I did.

Because over the years we moved to many different homes, I learned to take the system apart and put it all back together for our listening enjoyment. The interesting part about my being able to assemble a stereo system and dial in the equalizer is that I'm deaf in my right ear. I'm thinking my husband allowed me to do whatever I thought was correct and then fixed it without so much as one derogatory remark.

Throughout the years, I've encountered many people fitting the description of a tweeter or a woofer. They would be the not-so-easy-to-get-along-with people. When I think of tweeters, chirping birds do come to mind. I had a couple of women friends who were tweeters—always talking and never listening. I'd feel like I had the life sucked out of me by the time they left the room. They were coworkers, neighbors, churchgoers, and/or even fellow choir members. Nothing was ever right with their environment. They seemed to be in a constant flux, thinking this or that should be changed. At least that's how I perceived them.

The tweeters are always ready for an exciting adventure and are easy to spot a mile away. Entering a room for them is an event accompanied by high-pitched chatter and a giggle or two after each sentence. I have always found myself attracted to a tweeter and yet exhausted by their extended presence. They usually wear bright-colored, patterned blouses and often carried very large handbags filled with everything they might ever need.

Once I roomed with a tweeter at a Christian retreat. It was a very entertaining experience that I shall never forget. We shared a room with two double beds and one bathroom. I packed lightly with one sizeable suitcase for clothes and a smaller one for toiletries. My friend had two large suitcases, one small makeup case, and three shopping bags filled with all kinds of stuff. Out of the bag, she pulled several hairbrushes, two hairdryers, two curling irons, large bottles of shampoo, tubes of conditioners, a bottle of aspirin, and three extra-large boxes of toothpaste. When I asked her why in the world she brought all the extra stuff, she looked at me very innocently and told me that she always brought extra for the gal who would forget one thing or another. That was something I had never thought of: the other person's needs. Many of my friends today are tweeters. It's an adventure and a blessing to have a tweeter for a friend. They are very generous people caring for others all the time.

Woofers are very different. They're the loudmouths who talk over everyone, usually bragging about all their achievements and boasting of their talents. Mostly, they intimidated and overwhelmed me. Whatever I talked about, they had previously experienced. Wherever I traveled, they had already been. It was difficult to be in a room with a woofer. They were like barking dogs.

My first husband's father was a woofer. I was eighteen when I met him, and he scared me to death. His presence overshadowed everything and everyone. My mistake in our first year of marriage was trying to emulate his behavior so that I would be accepted. I found out that woofers do not like to be outdone.

During the year before my first marriage, I wanted to have a garden, so my boyfriend plowed and disked a small plot of ground on the Jake

Zobel Farm, a fifty-acre ranch owned by my father-in-law and farmed for hay. I planted tomatoes, peppers, cucumbers, and cantaloupe in my lovely little garden. I especially loved cantaloupe. I bragged to my father-in-law, a farmer for over twenty years, about how I could grow better vegetables than he could. I was being playful. To me, it was a game, just something to laugh and talk about. I then forgot about the contest regarding the garden.

A couple of months passed and it was time to check on my garden and its vegetables. To my horror, everything in the garden was ruined. The beautiful cantaloupes were full of bite marks. I was crushed. What could have happened? When I mentioned it to my first husband's parents, my father-in-law, the woofer, roared with wicked laughter. He explained that he was not about to be outdone by a young girl and her garden, so he opened the gate to the wire fence we had put around the garden to keep out the rabbits. I didn't like him much at that time, and I certainly didn't laugh. He was actually angry about the whole situation. He told his wife that unless I apologized to him for my disrespectful behavior, he would not attend the wedding. This would be my first experience at humbling myself and apologizing for something I felt was not my fault. My boyfriend told me if I would apologize this time, he would never ask me to apologize again. He said that his mother was really upset. I loved his mom, so I apologized.

When I was young, I didn't know how to deal with such people, but as I grew older, I learned that tweeters and woofers are just looking for attention. They can't be changed, and I certainly wouldn't try. They are what they were born to be. The best action is to understand what they are, pray for them, and walk away. Some people are just on this earth to serve as a warning to others. I like to think of woofers and tweeters as fillers of life making the world a more interesting place. We are to love one another without wishing they were different. They may never change, but we can. It's not our place to condemn, criticize, or complain.

My song of praise: "Humble Thyself in the Sight of the Lord" by Bob Hudson.
Bible quote: (Luke 18:14 NAS) "For everyone who exalts himself shall be humbled, but he who humbles himself shall be exalted."

CHAPTER 6

Sound Check

Sound is all around us. As we go through our everyday lives, we are subjected to sound, whether pleasant or harsh, soft or loud. The dictionary presents this explanation of the word *sound*: "A vibratory disturbance capable of being heard." Music is sound created by instruments and voice.

My instrument of choice, other than my voice, is a piano. It's interesting to know that most pianos are manufactured and tuned in the same way, yet they all have a unique sound. The sound from a player piano is different from a concert grand, whether by design or alteration. What I mean by "alteration" is when someone purposely changes the construction. I only know of one person who did that to a piano. My friend attached thumbtacks to the hammers of her piano so that when the keys were played, the hammers struck the piano strings, thereby creating a sound similar to the honky-tonk music played in the western bars of the old John Wayne movies. She used eighty-eight thumbtacks. She altered her piano for a sound that pleased her.

My growing years were spent in a country farmhouse on Cooper Street about twelve miles from the nearest town: Cato, New York. We moved from the city of Auburn to the country when I was in fourth grade. The living conditions were cramped and basic. We had no modern conveniences for the first two years. My grandparents moved in with us but only stayed a couple of years. Dad created an apartment for them by using half the downstairs of our house, which cramped a family of five. After they left, more construction gave us back the full house. Their leaving also gave us all their furniture and, most importantly, the old, brown, upright piano, which was promptly moved to the backroom.

The "backroom," as we unceremoniously called it, was a thirty-foot by twenty-foot room attached at the back of the house. Attached to that backroom was the only bathroom we had for the first seven months we lived there. It was a two-hole outhouse. When spring arrived, my dad built a luxurious outhouse about five hundred feet from the house and tore down the old one. The new outhouse had three holes: small, medium, and large. It also had a window adorned with flowered curtains.

Our family used the backroom for everything. The floor was cement, and the walls were unfinished. There was no heat during the winter. During the summer, the only air-conditioning came from a breeze flowing through two windows on opposite walls. Fallen trees that my dad and older brother hauled from the woods were sawn into logs with an old two-man crosscut saw and split into firewood. Evidence of the wood we split was shown in the nicks and chunks of cement missing from the floor. Dad slaughtered chickens on a log stump in the corner. We played table tennis on my grandma's antique, oval, dining-room table (corner shots were interesting). That oak table with the glass-claw feet sadly met its demise one winter when our family ran out of wood for the furnace.

All our relatives would come to the country on various occasions throughout the summer. They gathered in the backroom and drank beer from a keg cooling in a metal washtub filled with ice. The same washtub we all took baths in. We danced around the center pole that held up the roof. I even tried roller-skating around the poll, but the metal wheels got caught in the holes of the cement floor. My dad bought a booth from an old diner, painted it yellow, and installed it under one of the windows. That's where all the poker games were played. It was a famous backroom.

The best part of the backroom for me was that old piano. It sat against the outside wall through cold winters with temperatures well below zero and hot summers with temperatures above one hundred degrees and 100 percent humidity. The piano was so far out of tune it was difficult to know what an octave should sound like. It was so gruesome to hear that my dad gave up playing. I would listen to the radio and try to play a simple tune to match the sound. It seemed impossible. Because we had no extra money to get it tuned, it stayed unlovable.

One day as I sat at my beloved piano trying to play a song, I decided that I would open it up and take a look at how it was made. I lifted the front panel and slid it back until its two metal pegs on each side caught in the slots of the piano's side panels, allowing it to stay open. I sat on the bench and stared, fascinated by what was before me.

There were a lot of strings connected to square bolts. The strings to the left were wider in diameter than the strings to the right. It looked like a large guitar. I reached in and touched the strings, ran my hand across the strings, and plucked them with my finger. I was surprised and delighted that I had discovered the secret hidden behind the wooden panel. Each string had a different sound when I plucked it. I thought about it and decided if I tightened or loosened the string by turning the square bolt, I could change the sound.

I had the brilliant idea that just maybe I could tune it. I went to my dad's toolbox and grabbed some tools. I tried a screwdriver, several wrenches, and pliers of different sizes, without success. There had to be something that would fit over the square bolts.

I went to my bedroom and rummaged through my desk drawers, finding nothing. I pulled out the flat box that I kept under the bed and shuffled through all the odd items I had saved since moving from the city. Finally, I found the tool that I hoped would work: my old skate key! The skate key was extremely important to me, because without it, my skates were useless. It was the only tool that could be used to tighten or loosen the skates to my shoes. I kept the key on a string around my neck while I skated so I wouldn't lose it. Even though the skates were gone, I couldn't part with the key. To lose it would mean no skating, ever.

I snatched the key from the rest of my collectables and ran down the stairs, heading toward the backroom. It was just as I suspected: the skate key fit around the square bolts perfectly. I could tighten or loosen the strings and change the sound of the note being played. I pulled out my plastic flute, the instrument that I had learned to play in fifth-grade music class, and corrected middle C. Then I adjusted all the strings up and down one note until I made an octave. Now that's what I call a sound check!

I played that piano for six years. In winter, I would wear gloves to play until my fingers were stiff from the cold. That was a long time ago, but the memories are stored in my heart. I had to play that piano, so I tuned it until it sounded good to me. My parents paid for a few lessons, but it was already too late. I only played my way, by ear. Although the lessons did teach me the basics that later in life helped me to sing.

Singing is different from playing an instrument. A person can be taught to play an instrument. Whether it sounds good or bad, they can still play the instrument. Singing takes somewhat of a natural ability. You either want to sing or you don't. It would actually surprise some people to learn that they have a pleasant voice and could present it in an acceptable fashion. I've always been able to sing, and most importantly I wanted to sing. To this day, something in my soul needs to escape my lips, presenting some obscure tune in the form of a hum, a whistle, or soft air. Most of the time, I'm not even aware it's happening.

I have a good *ear* for music. I learned the songs Mom sang and the songs Dad played on the piano. Therefore, it was natural for me to recognize certain melodies. When I was in ninth grade, I auditioned for the senior-high chorus. At the audition, the music teacher asked if I could read music. I answered yes. Well, I could, sort of. I did have those few lessons in fifth grade. She handed me the sheet music for the song "No Man Is an Island." It just so happened that I knew the melody. I can't tell you why I knew that song, but I did. She played the piano and I sung the melody. I was in the chorus.

I learned a great deal from my choir director in high school. That's where the love for music was instilled in my heart. I had many opportunities to perform in Gilbert and Sullivan operettas. She taught me to sing solos by taking me to Syracuse University to compete and be adjudicated. She put me in a trio with two other gals and allowed us to perform at various luncheons and banquets. She helped us to build confidence and pride in what we accomplished. She was one of the great teachers in my life. Her name was Mrs. Downer, and she was anything but that. When she directed our chorus, she bounced all over the stage. That's just one of many joyful memories I have of her.

After high school, music was not high on my list of priorities. A husband, three children, and a farm filled my life for fifteen years. My daughter found the music I seemed to have lost. She excelled in the ability to play the flute, along with various other instruments. The gift of voice was also given to her. Her music filled the house for years, while my inner music seemed buried.

As the years passed with life's good and bad situations, I found music once again in a most unlikely place. A church! That's surprising because I was not a regular church attendee. I was a retired Catholic. Who would have thought that music would fill my heart and become my love again at a nondenominational church in Modesto, California, 3,050 miles from my hometown of Cato, New York?

The greatest gift from God was not any of the jobs my second husband and I found but a church we visited. Thanks to a wonderful couple who bribed us with breakfast, we decided to attend a Sunday service. Dave and I never attended church; as I mentioned, the last time I went to church regularly was when I was a child. It was the beautiful music sung by the choir that lifted my heart and drew me back each Sunday. After attending for several months, my husband and I became members. The best decision I ever made a couple of years later was to join the celebration choir.

I remember the first night I started as a member of the choir. What a sound check! I walked down the hall on my way to the choir room, turned the corner, and stopped dead in my tracks. The sound that filled my ears was music surely sung by a hundred angels. Tears filled my eyes and a slight foreboding tingled in my chest as I reached for the door handle. As beautiful as the music was, I knew that I didn't know how to sing those songs. The only church songs I knew were in Latin. I could read music, but years had passed since I had sung in the college choir back in New York. And we didn't sing about God. Where was that old confidence of mine? I knew that I was partially out of my element, but I faced the door, turned the handle, and stepped into the choir room.

Upon entering, I felt sixty sets of eyes on me. I was asked by the music secretary what I sang, and I responded, "I sing alto." I was handed a binder full of music and directed toward the right side of the choir. I didn't know anyone, but the faces looked familiar because I had spent two years sitting in the congregation and staring up at the choir. My only thought was, *What in the world am I thinking?* However, it was too late; I couldn't back out.

I'm an alto

The sound of my name seemed to float over the heads of all the altos as I approached the group. I noticed Martha waving from the back row and beckoning me to join her. Needless to say, I was quite relieved that she was there. After all, she was the one who visited me once a week in my office at the church, always inviting me to join the choir. Martha was a great help with the music, but more importantly, she made me feel comfortable and accepted. As we sang, I listened for her voice and matched her tone. Even though her voice was different from mine, our sounds blended as we sang. The choir was like an orchestra filled with unique instruments all blending to create beautiful music. One voice or instrument is not better than the other, just different. Within a couple of years, I learned many great Christian hymns. These melodies linger in my heart and escape my lips periodically with no warning. They are beautiful songs about Jesus and how He loves us.

What exactly is a sound check? It's the preparation that takes place before a concert, speech, or similar performance. Most often, the performer and the sound crew will run through a small portion of the upcoming show on the venue's sound system to make sure that the sound is clear and at the right volume and tonal frequencies. It's important that an orchestra or a choir has a perfect blend. Listening to a performance by a jazz band wouldn't be enjoyable if the only instrument we heard was the saxophone. A blend of all the instruments is more pleasant. Likewise, in a choir, no one wants to hear Maggie, the soprano belting out high notes louder than the rest of the voices. I have heard that one voice high above the others, ruining the blend and, ultimately, the performance.

I learned that it was far more difficult to sing in a choir than to play the piano for my own enjoyment. While playing the piano, I was one person making sound. Within a choir, there are many voices making sound and there is a blend that has to be accomplished. I learned to listen to the sound around me, to understand its meaning, and to adjust my position. I learned this not only with music and other singers but with people who have influenced me throughout life. There is a reason I have two ears and one mouth. To me, life is one big sound check.

My song of praise: "Unto Thee, Oh Lord, Do I Lift up My Voice" by unknown.
Bible quote: (Proverbs 16:23 NAS) "The heart of the wise teaches his mouth, and adds persuasiveness to his lips …"

SECTION 3

Disappointments

CHAPTER 7

Hear the Harmony

Harmony is that wonderful sound that comes from two or three blended voices. Harmony is also present in a choir with its pleasing combination of parts or elements in a song. It's a combination and progression of chords in musical structure. In music, there are melody, harmony, and sometimes discord. Oh no, not discord.

Don't you think that everything in music is like everything in life, with its order and confusion, softness and harshness, fast rhythm and slow beats on a drum, and finally chaos and harmony? These elements exist within family units, in places of worship, and at the workplace. Because I've sung as an alto in many choirs, I've learned to recognize harmony in music. It hasn't been that easy to recognize it in life. More often than not, it may get hidden by complacency and end up being unrecognizable. When we just don't care about anything, forget to work on what is important, and take harmony for granted, we may be in jeopardy of losing it.

Chaos ensues where harmony or unity is absent. I listened to a concert by the Boston Philharmonic Orchestra and was intrigued by the sound it made as each instrument warmed up in preparation for the performance. An accurate description of how I felt would be nervous and agitated. I didn't want to hear the harsh noise coming from the stage. It was hurtful to my ears. The horns were blaring; the flutes were going up and down the musical scale; the string instruments were plucking and bowing; and occasionally, the kettledrum would sound out a *boom, boom, boom.* The dictionary gives this meaning to chaos: "The behavior of systems that follow deterministic laws but appear random and unpredictable." That definition was exactly what was happening in the auditorium.

After a few minutes, the violinist walked on stage and stood in front of his chair as an indication to begin the performance. All the harsh noise stopped. The audience became silent. Only one note could be heard. A distinct "A" penetrated the silence. A beautiful, clear sound was played by the oboe. The violinist pointed to each section of the orchestra and, one by one, each instrument tuned to the "A." Soon, all sections were in sync. Unity ensued while the whole audience seemed to hold their breaths; order out of chaos was apparent. The conductor walked on stage, took his place on the podium, raised his baton, and initiated a wonderful performance. Melodies and harmonies floated throughout the auditorium.

As with music, life is filled with symphonies encompassing harmonies, melodies, and dissonance. Around the small village of Cato, New York, where I grew up, there were many farms housing large families. A couple of my friends in school came from some of those large families. It was always a treat to visit them and share dinner.

One of my friends had four brothers and four sisters. Once, I was lucky to be invited to their house for dinner after school. Their dining-room table accommodated eight to ten chairs with a smaller table for the young children. Compared to my one sister and one brother, this family was huge. Before we ate dinner, there was pandemonium in the kitchen and total chaos throughout the house. Wonderful scents of roast beef and apple pie floated through the air. Pots were coming and going from the stove. Dishes rattled and silverware plunked as the table was set. Glasses were being filled with ice and water. The mother directed every move just as a conductor directed a symphonic orchestra. The sound was as if one hundred chattering geese landed on the front lawn.

Finally, one voice over the chaos could be heard. "Come and get it!" Everyone rushed to the dining room and began discussing everything from yesterday's homework to Annie's lost sock, the plans to play Scrabble after dessert, and something about Aunt Margaret's visit next week. Chairs scraped the floor as they were pulled from the table. Their mom, being the last to enter the room, pulled her chair out and sat down, taking the hand of each person next to her. Silence filled the room as she thanked the Lord and asked for blessings on the food. This was my favorite house to visit. It was easy to hear the harmony.

Not every home is harmonic. Not every home is a happy dwelling place. Not every home is filled with love and peace. There are homes that rock with anger and shouts of hatred. Some homes are filled with drugs and alcohol abuse. Some homes are filled with sexual abuse. I only know a couple of homes that grew such dissonance. One was my mother's, and ironically one was mine.

My mother grew up with a father that sexually abused her. She never told her mother; she just dealt with it in her own way, which was keeping quiet and avoiding her father. She told me that if she had told her mother what was happening, it would have hurt her too much. Pictures of my mother at a young age showed a very mature young lady. She was tall with beautiful, black, curly hair. Her eyes were green with brown flecks, the color we call "hazel." Sometimes when I'm washing my face or combing my hair, I look at my eyes in the mirror and see Mom looking back at me. So much that we know now regarding abuse wasn't known two generations ago. People just dealt with the hurt and pain.

From the stories I've heard, my mother's father was a mean man who spent most of his time sitting in the basement drinking beer, especially when guests would arrive. He was a policeman in a small town in central New York. He was a World War I veteran who died later in life from the residual effects of mustard gas used by the Germans in 1917. I'm sure he had many issues to deal with and no understanding of how to do so. I was too young to remember Louis, but I grew to love his wife, Marie. Everyone called her "Rie." She was my favorite grandmother.

As a married woman with three children, I had to deal with many negative aspects of my life. I loved my first husband, but he had issues. He didn't know how to deal with his own inadequacies and the hurts caused by others. So he drank. At first, it was fun to spend time at the local hotels drinking and dancing and socializing. It was our Saturday night out. We both spent a lot of time away from home, consuming a great deal of beer. We saw no harm in what we did. Because I grew up in a family atmosphere of drinking, it seemed almost normal to me. I remember my mother telling me on one of the nights my husband missed dinner that someday I would not be so happy with him. I would argue that he wasn't doing anything wrong. I should have listened to my mother. His late arrivals for dinner grew to be a habit and did in fact become very annoying. Trouble began when I decided that I was done with the drinking and spending time at the various bars. He told me that he did not have trouble with his drinking—I did.

I was young and inexperienced, so I endured for several years as his drinking began to take over his life. I could not solve this problem; I just didn't know how. After fourteen years, a great deal of grief, and thousands of prayers, I gave up. Our marriage traveled on a destructive path that eventually ended in divorce. I found my plans destroyed and the harmony gone.

Life is a learning process that each human must endure. I say "endure" because the learning is not always comfortable. I'm an alto and I know what harmony is and how it applies to music. Applying it to people continues to be somewhat of a mystery to me. It's not always easy to be kind and gentle, to find unity in chaos, or to create harmony out of discord. I've had nearly a lifetime to practice, yet still I struggle to be at peace. I have learned to accept what is and to move on to a different song. I know a thousand different songs. "Pick one," my heart tells me.

My song of praise: "Make Me a Blessing" by George Schuler and Ira Wilson.

Bible quote: (1 Corinthians 1:10 NAS) "Now I exhort you, brethren, by the name of our Lord Jesus Christ, that you all agree, and there be no divisions among you, but you be made complete in the same mind and in the same judgment."

CHAPTER 8

Whole Notes with Too Many Dots

For me, there are three basic parts to music: notes, rhythm, and tempo. A written note has a note value, a code that determines the note's relative duration. There are five basic types of notes: whole notes, half notes, quarter notes, eighth notes, and sixteenth notes. They are all put together on a staff to create a song. Therefore, when you look at written music, you see lots of lines, shapes, and words that tell you what sound to sing and how long to hold each sound.

Rhythm is made up of sounds and silences. The sounds are the notes, and the silences are rests. They are put together to form a pattern of sounds, which are repeated to create a rhythm. Rhythm can have a steady beat or fluctuating beats. Some may be stronger, longer, shorter, or softer than others. In a single piece of music, a composer can use many different rhythms. If you listen for it, you can find a rhythm just about anywhere: in a basketball being dribbled, raindrops hitting on a tin roof, high heels clacking on a marble floor in an office building as women rush to board an elevator, or waves crashing on an ocean beach.

To add more confusion, there's the matter of how fast or slow to play all the different rhythms. Tempo is the speed of the music. It's a steady, constant pulse, like a clock ticking. Tempo can be slow, fast, or in-between. It also can change during a song. The tempo of music influences how we interpret the sound and how we react emotionally. The same piece of music will sound differently if you play it slower or faster. The names of five tempos are adagio (very slow), andante (slow), moderate (medium), allegro (fast), and presto (very fast).

There's one musical term I haven't mentioned: the dot. Often in written music there will be dots after the notes. A dot that is placed after a note increases the duration of the note. It is increased by half of the basic note. For example, a dotted half note will be held two counts of its own and one more count, equaling a total of three. A whole note with a dot will be held six counts instead of four.

Notes, rhythms, tempos, dots, and rests are significant in understanding music. They are also significant in the ebb and flow of life. As we travel through life, we use a distinct tempo and rhythm. Sometimes, we are fast, and other times, we are slow. We have dreams and goals that take a while to realize. Often, they take too long, and many times, our dreams can get in the way of reality. We become so focused on what we want to do that we can't see what is needed. An example of using too many dots and holding a note too long would be staying in a painful marriage or holding on to the security of a job despite the presence of unfair practices. It's difficult to know when to let go. How do you let go of a dream? There are times when we just can't. The dream consumes us, and we become obsessed with its realization. I had a dream and it disintegrated right before my very eyes, yet I survived. If I may, let me explain.

I had never had any trouble accomplishing goals and getting what I wanted out of life, until I moved to California with my husband. After being a member of the church choir and sitting in the alto section for a couple of years, I found myself yearning to participate more. I wanted to be a bigger part of the music department that I so loved. Sunday morning services offered plenty of opportunities to sing. There were two services consisting of choir music, worship music with a team at the beginning of the service, solo music, piano, organ, and sometimes a whole orchestra performing on Sundays. Each Sunday seemed to be a concert as the beautiful and inspiring music filled the auditorium with praises to God. The congregation loved the music. I was in love with the music, and I wanted to present it in any way I could, in all ways if possible. I wanted to sing on the worship team. I wanted to be a part of small groups. I wanted to sing solos with and without the choir as backup. I wanted it all and got none of it. I was only allowed to sing in the choir. My wants became an obsession. This was my whole note with too many dots. Year after year passed, and the fact that I was not included in *church special music* ate my lunch.

It's very interesting what a person does when a dream becomes an obsession. I listened to many singers within our choir and decided that I could do the same, perhaps even better. Unfortunately, or maybe fortunately, my choir director did not see it my way. Today, I understand, but twenty years ago, I did not.

As I reflect back, the soloists within the choir sang well with confidence, always presenting themselves with poise and grace. They sang all the great solos with no fear. I wanted so much to sing some of those songs, but fear kept me from asking the choir director for help. Instead, I complained to others. I asked in bitterness why the same people always got to sing. I thought the choir director should ask me to sing. I just knew he could hear my voice, because I sang loudly at every practice and he did look at me from time to time. Now that I think of it, he probably couldn't believe that he was hearing a loud alto singing above everyone else's voice. In my mind, I thought that he should think, *Wow! I really need her to sing for me.* I spent a lot of time trying to get his attention.

In my mind, wanting something and needing something were entirely different. If he needed me to sing and I made a mistake, I was forgiven. But if I whined about wanting to sing and made a mistake after he'd given in, I was considered a failure. I was not into failure. Because fear had me in its grip, I couldn't approach my director.

After a couple of years, the need to sing became a burn within me. I wanted to sing on the worship team. No one asked me. When the director put together a group of women to sing special music, I wanted to be a part of it. I wasn't asked. I was part of the choir for three years, and I knew all the ladies who sang. I listened to them sing wonderful music for two seasons. I also listened to them grumble in the restroom before the services. They were doing something I would have given just about anything to do, and they were complaining about it. They would say the music was too hard or the alto part was boring, or they would ask, "Why do we have to sing the same old songs all the time?" My heart was broken. When they practiced before a Sunday service, I would sit on the pew and listen with tears in my eyes. In wanting something so badly, I could hardly think of anything else. I questioned myself constantly. Maybe I was too fat. Maybe I didn't have the right clothes. Maybe I just wasn't pretty enough. Maybe I was too old. What was wrong with me?

One night after choir practice, I finally worked up enough nerve to ask the choir director what I would have to do in order to sing a solo. He suggested voice lessons and a move to the soprano section to learn to sing melody. He also suggested that I get two tape recorders and a soundtrack of a song. Play the song on one recorder and listen to it with headphones while singing and recording my voice with the other. Next, play the machine that recorded my voice. If I stayed on key and it sounded good, then I would be ready. He added that it might take one year or five years.

I know what you're thinking: *Is this woman nuts? Did she really do that?* I did. For one year, I practiced. I purchased twenty tapes and learned each song. I even recorded a tape of my voice singing various songs and gave it to him. His response was less than encouraging. I was begging for help, guidance, and mentoring and got nothing. I was like a child wanting some toy that my parents would not purchase for me. I tried everything I could to be a soloist in that choir and to sing in small groups.

I was obsessed by the fact that I could not sing, yet I wasn't brave enough to ask. You see, I had never failed at anything I tried to do, except this time! No matter what I did, I was not included in that special group that was allowed to sing special music in church. Each time I would hear someone sing a solo of a song that I liked, I would purchase the tape and practice until I knew the song and could sing it. Problem was there was no place for me to sing the song. I just didn't understand; therefore, I became angry and combative. I felt the music dying in me. Four years had passed, and I was just another soprano singing with a bunch of other high voices.

I think it's possible as a member of a music ministry in a church to go in one of two directions. One direction would be to honor, love, and sing for the Lord, thereby allowing the congregation to be blessed by the beautiful music. The other direction would be to entertain for the applause and self-gratification. Either direction can be a slippery slope toward disaster if taken to extreme. As I reflect upon the past, I think that my motives for singing were for self-gratification. I was confused about the ministry side of the music department. Maybe my choir director knew of my desires to sing and felt that I was not a mature enough Christian to handle that slippery slope. Or he just wasn't aware of me at all. Perhaps to him, I was one of seventy-five other choir members. After all, I wasn't the only person who wanted to be recognized and used.

Occasionally, guest speakers filled in for our senior pastor when he vacationed. One particular Sunday, I had the opportunity to listen to a sermon by such a guest speaker. The subject of his sermon was about church ministries and those who served in them. He talked about people who wanted to be a part of a ministry that was not available to them. No matter how hard they tried or how long they hung in there, they were not chosen to serve. That was me!

The speaker continued that a number of individuals were so sure it was God leading them in a certain direction they prayed about it constantly. They were consumed with the dream and dwelled on it all the time. They talked to others and became angry and bitter because they were not chosen. That was me!

"And they waited," he said, "waited with no answer. They were eaten up with their own wants and desires and never thought that perhaps God had something different in mind, a different direction. Even though many prayers were initiated, still God did not say yes." The speaker then asked the audience, "When do you give up and ask God what He wants in your life?"

That was the last sentence I heard the speaker say. The sentence echoed in my mind as I sat completely unaware of the rest of his sermon. I only heard the question he asked. "When do you give up and ask God what He wants in your life?" Today, I can still hear those words. I spent almost seven years wanting something that God did not want for me. I don't mind telling you that it hurt. Even today it hurts a bit. It hurts because I felt the need to be included and was not. I felt that I had wasted years of my life chasing after something that God did not want for me.

I was wrong in my attitude and actions. At that time during my life, I just needed to be needed. I moved from the east coast to the west and left my family three thousand miles behind. I had new friends who didn't know the actual me. I was afraid of all the newness and strangeness in my life, so I hid my real self and reflected arrogance. I didn't need to be that way.

After being in the choir for a couple of years, I grew to love the music and the music director. I wanted to sing for him. I should have wanted to sing for the Lord. I wanted my choir director to know that I agreed with all that he believed in. I placed him on a very high pedestal. So high that I couldn't reach him. He knew nothing of my feelings. As I reflect back, I realize that he was correct in not putting me in a position where I may have fallen on my face. He knew that I wasn't capable of doing what I wanted to do. I just wish that he had taken the time then to help me understand. I don't think I would have been quite as angry and hurt. I was learning a new way to live, and at times, it was uncomfortable and confusing. He knew best; I just wasn't patient enough. I was angry for a long time, but not anymore. What I feel now is embarrassment at my behavior. The one thing I had to learn was humility. I just wasn't as great as I thought I was.

My story of the whole note with too many dots doesn't end with total disaster. However, I didn't turn my life around after hearing that one special speaker that asked whether or not I had prayed and asked for God's guidance. I had one more plan. I promised myself that this would be the last effort I would make to get noticed. I just knew that this would be the time he would ask me to sing on the worship team or even sing a solo. It was my plan for my gain. It was my plan for attention. I would finally be thought of as a wonderful singer. Can you believe this? I'm here to tell you that it didn't turn out the way I planned—it turned out better! It has only taken me fifteen years to realize it.

My song of praise: "One Day at a Time" by Marijohn Wilkin and Kris Kristofferson.

Bible quote: (James 4:3 NAS) "You ask and do not receive, because you ask with wrong motives, so that you may spend it on your pleasures."

CHAPTER 9

Music, Music, Music

"Let's call ourselves Spice of Life," one of the gals in the group suggested. I liked that name. We were all different in age and size, we all had different backgrounds, and we all came from different churches. We were spicy. It was the most fun I've ever had with a group of women, and best of all, we were singing. We went to just about every nursing home and retirement center in the city where I lived. We sang twenty songs; ten were oldies but goodies and ten were Christian. It took us just about an hour. We were a semi-polished group, but it didn't start out that way.

As I explained in the last chapter, I had devised a plan to get some notice and attention from my choir director because I wanted so badly to sing solos. My dream, or at this point my obsession, wasn't quite dead yet. I thought that I would get together a group of singers and visit nursing homes. When I think back, I don't know where that idea came from. I didn't know anyone in a nursing home or even where there were any nursing homes to sing in. But I went with the idea and asked my choir director if I could pass around a sheet during choir and get some signups. Quite a few people were interested until they found out that the director was not included. That was okay with me. I didn't really want him to sing with us. I just wanted him to notice me.

The first practice brought two people and one of them was iffy, but I went with it. I purchased an instrumental background tape of four spiritual songs in the style of a famous rock-and-roller. The only gal who came to practice memorized the songs with me and we presented them to our first audience. The one thing you need to remember is that I was not familiar with Christian gospel songs, and I was pretty much still an alto. I think it was in the middle of the second song when the white-haired woman in the back yelled out, "You *ain't singin'* that right, honey!" I decided right then and there that I would grab the church hymnal and figure out how those old songs needed to be sung.

During that first mini-concert at the nursing home, my knees were shaking and I could hardly hold on to the microphone that was plugged into my karaoke machine. But something happened, something that would change my life. These people were very loving and accepting of what I was doing. They were certainly a captive audience and very forgiving of my feeble attempts to entertain. The first time is always just that: *the first time.* I knew that if I were to continue, I would need help. Did I pray about it? Nope, I did not. Not yet.

My little group of two expanded when I asked one of the sopranos who sat next to me in choir if she ever sang in a small group. She was exactly the right person to ask. She had sung in a trio at her prior church. She also added that in her Sunday school class there was another gal who played a mean accordion and she might be interested in joining us. Guess where I went the following Sunday. I visited the Sunday school class and listened to some wonderful music. I asked her if she would like to practice with us and play piano. She told me she would love to. Now I had four, including myself. We decided to meet every Wednesday and practice. I invited one of the tenors from choir to join us. He was a wonderful addition to our group, and he brought along his friend who happened to sing bass. What a group this was.

We called ourselves Spice of Life, and that is exactly what we were. One gal played the piano and accordion. The first song I heard her play on the piano was "Beer Barrel Polka" by Jaromir Vejvoda. It was an emotional experience for me because that was the first song I learned to play, thanks to my dad. That was the first song I could play using octaves. She knew all the old songs my dad played, and she played them with the same excitement. The other gal from choir had this wonderful second soprano voice. There wasn't anything she couldn't sing. She had tons of music and tapes that we used in practice. We would sit around her dining-room table for an hour, learning our parts. Most importantly, before we began, we would pray. Hmm, that was a new concept for me. When we finished practice, we would have coffee and something wonderful that she had created in her oven just for us. It was a special time for me. She taught me a great deal about relying on the Lord to handle situations. I was learning about ministry and music. We sang for Sunday school classes at the church quite frequently. Specifically, we sang for the pastor in charge of the seniors. They knew all the old songs and sang right along with us.

Eventually, we traded in my old karaoke and purchased some high-quality equipment that helped our voices blend. One hot summer day in central California, we were to perform at a birthday party for a gentleman who I think was turning eighty. He wanted only popular songs of the 1940s and 1950s. We could do that, except we weren't sure we wanted to perform at a party. So when I was asked how much we would charge, I answered with one hundred dollars. I thought for sure they would never pay that much. Well, I was wrong. So there we were, on a makeshift stage in ninety-eight degrees with our matching polyester, white, long-sleeved blouses; silk scarves; and black pants, sweating and singing like we knew what we were doing. We laughed a lot over that mini concert.

We made music. There was a particular song my dad played on the piano that our piano player knew. Every time she played it, the old memories would flood my heart. The song started with, "Put another nickel in, in that nickelodeon." The name of the song is "Music, Music, Music," written by Stephan Weiss and Bernie Baum.

Music is sound usually produced by instruments or voices that are arranged or played in order to create an effect. There are many different types of music, and it can be divided into many genres in different ways. These classifications are often arbitrary and closely related styles overlap. It may be argued that generic classification of musical styles is not possible in any logically consistent way and classification sets limitations and boundaries that hinder the development of music. When I looked up the classifications of music on the Internet, there were well over one hundred different types. Actually, I once heard that there were only two types of music: county and western. This may be true to some, but not all are in agreement. I was raised with music that was popular in my parents' life because they heard it on the radio and played it on the piano. This was music from the 1940s big-band era. This music I was able to share with the elderly residents at retirement centers.

Many outside factors can affect our emotions, such as music, movies, friends, books, television shows, something said, and even food. One of these factors is obviously music. Even without words, music can make us joyful or depressed, energized or sleepy. Think of the last time a song really moved you or meant something to you. Listening to and playing music stimulates many different sections of the brain, affecting us physically as well. Why are we as humans so connected to music?

Making music is one of our most basic instincts. There's a reason why we refer to music as the universal language: there's been no known human culture without it. Dancing and music came before agriculture and possibly even before language. I have recently read that some bone flutes were found in Europe dating back fifty-three thousand years. It has been suggested that whale music and human music have much in common, even though our evolutionary paths have not intersected. This implies that music may predate human existence. Rather than being the inventors of music, as we claim to be, we may actually be latecomers to the musical scene.

We begin life being affected by music; babies first begin to respond to music while still in the womb. Whether or not it's true, everyone has heard that playing classical music for your baby supposedly helps him or her become smarter. Many studies have been done regarding this. Researchers have also found that the playing of soft background music or a mother's humming actually helps premature babies. Those who are subjected to the music tend to gain weight faster and are able to leave hospitals earlier than those who aren't. Another fact that I know is true is this: music in a dairy barn will help cows relax and enable them to produce more milk. When my first husband and I were farming, we always played some kind of music in the barn as we milked the cows. It was a peaceful experience for man and beast.

After singing at nursing homes for about a year, I asked the activity director if the residents enjoyed our music. I asked this because they didn't interact a whole lot with us while we were singing. Many of them left the room and they hardly ever applauded. The activity director told me that the residents did indeed remember us and often asked for us about a week after we left. Also, the activity director told me that the old spiritual hymns seemed to wake up a few of the residents. I was encouraged by that. Music does soothe the soul. Whenever our group would start to sing an old hymn, I would notice a few ladies in the back row start to tap their feet or their fingers. Just when I thought they were asleep, I would see recognition. Then there were the few seniors that would ask for hymns we never heard of. I would dig out the old church hymnal and search for the song. We could always count on our piano player to know exactly how to play it.

Over a period of fifteen years, many gals and guys joined and left our Spice of Life group. In the end, there were always the three of us, and eventually even that diminished when two of the gals moved away, leaving only me. What started out as a ploy to get attention turned into a ministry that filled my heart with many blessings. God had turned my obsession to sing solos into a ministry that touched hundreds of old souls. I thought I failed because I never got asked to sing a solo with the choir. Had the choir director asked me to sing, I would have been happy to just be a soloist singing a few songs every now and then. I am sure I never would have put together a group of loving people who wanted to sing and entertain the elderly.

I know what you're wondering. Did my choir director ever notice me and ask me to sing? He did not. He was responsible for teaching me many beautiful Christian songs and worship choruses that move around in my head all the time. I appreciate all the time he devoted to the music ministry at the church, and I have told him so. I'm thankful he never asked me to sing.

What's important is that I learned to listen to God. It was just like that special speaker said. "Ask the Lord what He wants you to do." God led me in the direction He wanted me to go. Actually, I think *dragged* would be a more appropriate verb. There were many side streets and dead ends taken and many lessons learned because I turned a deaf ear to God and concentrated on what I wanted. What I did out of spite, God turned into a blessing. I grew to love our audiences. That's how a few Sunday afternoons of singing turned into fifteen years. I soon forgot about singing solos at my church and ultimately lowered my choir director down from the very high pedestal where I had placed him.

Often I think of the many friends that sang with me. Don was the wonderful tenor who played guitar and sang "Mr. Bojangles" by Jerry Jeff Walker. Don left this earth too early to sing in the Lord's choir, and I've missed him. One gal with her lively accordion music entertains many retired people at campgrounds up and down the west coast. Another gal and her family members sing at retirement centers and church Sunday school classes every so often.

I reflect on the many residents we met who have since passed away: the woman who wanted my recording of music, the Italian man who shouted, "Bella! Bella!" after I sang, the lady who gave me a list of her favorite songs, and the ladies with the red hats who smiled for my camera. They felt so special that I would want to take their picture. I am thankful that God allowed me the opportunity to give my senior friends some pleasure while they were here.

My song of praise: "His Eye Is on the Sparrow" by Civilla D. Martin and Charles H. Gabriel.
Bible quote: (Proverbs 3:3 NAS) "Commit your works to the Lord, and your plans will be established."

Nursing Home

SECTION 4

Redirection

CHAPTER 10

Four / Four Time

In a musical score, the time signature appears at the beginning of the piece of music as a stacked number, such as 4/4, 3/4, or 2/4. The lower number indicates the note value, which represents one beat. The upper number indicates how many such beats there are in a measure. The most common simple time signatures are 2/4, 3/4, and 4/4. The time signature is important, as it gives us an indication of the tempo and rhythm of a song.

Four-four time is used most commonly in western popular music, blues, and country. "A Bicycle Built for Two," by Harry Dacre, is an example of a song written in four-four time. Three-four time is used for waltzes like the "Tennessee Waltz" by Redd Stewart and Pee Wee King. Two-four time is used for polkas like "Beer Barrel Polka" by Jaromir Vejvoda and marches like "The Washington Post March" by John Philip Sousa. When we sing or play a song, we need to know the rhythm and tempo. Otherwise, all music would sound the same. You wouldn't be able to tell the difference between a waltz and a polka. High-school bands would be marching to the country-western ballad of "Take Me Home, Country Roads" by John Denver, Taffy Nivert, and Bill Danoff. Timing is important in music. The variance in sound and presentation keep us entertained. Time signatures also have an influence on our lives.

When I travel, I often hear, "What time is it?" Needing to know the time of day seems paramount in our society. Most of us have a good idea of the time as it passes with every second and travels forward, seemingly to eat up our very existence. Time, when measured, is displayed many different ways with watches on our wrists, watches hanging around our necks on long chains, and even tiny watches in rings for our fingers. We seem preoccupied with the passing of time, evidenced by every home having at least one clock. I counted the timepieces in my house and came up with twenty. Almost every room in my home has a clock. There are the microwave, the coffee pot, the wall clock in the kitchen shaped like an apple, the antique living-room clock that sits on the fireplace mantle (not working), and the dining-room clock. I have a clock radio in the bedroom, an alarm clock in my husband's bathroom, three computers with clocks, the answering machine, a clock in each of our two cars, three watches belonging to my husband, and four watches of my own. We waste time; we spend time; we never have enough time; and the most often used phrase is the time-out.

Timing is everything in life and seems most elusive in its understanding with questions like "Is it time yet?" A phrase I most often use is "Where did the time go?" It seems I just closed my eyes for a minute and my three children were married with families of their own. I tell all my young friends, "Don't blink. Cherish the moments with your children because time is all too fleeting." Time is measured from the second to the minute, the hour, the day, the week, the month, and the year. Our year is divided into four seasons: spring, summer, autumn, and winter. The whole world, both civilized and uncivilized, understands the seasons of a year by celebrating each one uniquely. For me, each season has at least one holiday to celebrate: Easter in spring, Independence Day in summer, Thanksgiving in autumn, and

Christmas in winter. We travel through all four seasons every year of our lives.

Spring is a time of renewal and rebirth with another year approaching and its promise of change and greater success. We have the old list of New Year's resolutions tacked to the bulletin board in the office, reminding us of the excitement involved in fixing, changing, and rebuilding projects in our homes. In my home, I hear statements like "This is the year we'll finish staining the deck. I'll build a new herb garden. The shed can be painted and also the trim on the house. And oh, that front door can be replaced." The list goes on.

Plant life is emerging from deep winter's sleep. Brand-new leaves sprout on the trees with their color of fresh green. Flowers start to push through the ground, spotting the landscape with yellows and reds. Daisies pop to life everywhere. Each spring, I look forward to the daisies. I am reminded of when my husband and I first bought our

house in Oregon; spring was in full bloom and so were thousands of daisies in our backyard. It almost looked like a blanket of snow. The sun makes its appearance earlier in the day and hangs  around a little longer as the days pass. Winter is over. A new beginning is on the land.

Easter is a holiday when I celebrate Christ's escape from the grave, signifying a rebirth of the soul. Just like my tulip bulbs that lie deep in the cold soil during winter and then bloom in spring, I am invigorated by the sun's warmth and filled with desire and ambition, joy and anticipation. Spring is the time in our lives when we start families and begin to grow and mature. We are young and eager. We are alive and moving forward, feeling the constant beat of four-four time.

Summer brings growth to our lives as we settle into a rhythm of absorbing and reflecting, learning and teaching, while gaining maturity. We build our homes and fill them with our treasures of life. Our children are growing up, and so are we. The temperatures are warm, and the rains have subsided. Our gardens are planted, and they too are maturing with the promise of bounty. It's a time in our lives when we are moving slowly and more cautiously, going to a place where life is sure and comfortable.

I celebrate Independence Day on the Fourth of July with picnics, fireworks, and a sense of freedom. It's the time of year when eating outside on the patio becomes enjoyable and the grill gets a good workout. Trips to the area lakes and rivers are challenging as we entice the fish out of the waters with worms and other tidbits. We hike in the woods, walk on the ocean beaches, and watch the fluffy clouds roll by while swinging in the backyard hammock. We are happy and settled, absorbing life's bumps and joys much like the slightly different movement of a waltz played at three-quarter time.

As autumn approaches, summer feels all too fleeting, sometimes bringing an uncertainty of the future. It's a time in our lives when we start to slow down. A phrase that repeats itself is this: "I'm in the autumn of my life." It's a time when we think about life after kids. What'll we do when the nest we so carefully built is empty? The twigs separate and fall away because the leaves that are intertwined become dry and crumbly. The wind seems to be blowing in all directions, dislodging that nest from our safe limbs. The garden is dying, and the fruit is gone. It's the time of year when we put away the lawn chairs, the grill, the patio table and umbrella, the garden tools, and the lawn mower. We start to think of getting rid of stuff rather than accumulating more. Our lives are slipping out of our control. Retirement becomes the topic of discussion, and health or the lack of it becomes our main conversation. The career we held for many years has somehow lost its luster as we grow weary of the six o'clock commute. We find that we've arrived at a time in our lives when we reflect on all that we have accomplished.

Autumn is the third season of the year, a third phase of life that brings us to a time when we store memories. I remember the beauty of autumn in New York. Watching the leaves on the maple trees turn bright red, yellow, and orange is breathtaking. There is nothing more beautiful than driving through the Adirondack Mountains and seeing splashes of color throughout the forest. I grew up in the Finger Lakes region of central New York, and I never grew tired of autumn.

Autumn gives us the holiday of Thanksgiving. When I was a child, our family got together to share a huge dinner. We had turkey and stuffing, cranberries and cabbage salad, mashed potatoes and gravy, and apple pie. It was a day for serious eating. However, before we ate, we all stood around the table hand in hand, ready to make two statements. The first was what we were most sorry for, and the second was what we were most grateful for. It was an uncomfortable time for me, because I wanted to say something very meaningful. However, I was a child and innocent in my thinking. I didn't have too much that I was sorry for, and I was always grateful for the food. Today, I could make quite a list of sorrows and grateful blessings because I have lived many years and gone through many seasons. I am sorry for all the people I may have hurt as I traveled through life, and I'm grateful that I'm forgiven.

We talk to God, often thanking him for the blessings we have rather than asking Him for more. In the autumn of my life, I find that I want to be closer to God. I thank Him for the blessings of my beautiful children who have matured into happy, successful adults with children of their own. I thank Him for a husband who, after thirty years, still loves me with the same excitement we shared on our first date. I thank God for the beauty of it all, for the earth and the sky. I thank Him for my health and the health of my loved ones.

Autumn is my favorite time of the year. The hassle of my life has disappeared. I don't have to prove myself to anyone. I can relax and let my hair be white. My waste is not tiny anymore. Actually, it never was tiny. I can enjoy a dish of ice cream without counting the calories. The responsibility of raising children has passed. I am content with what I am. I want to sing a crazy song in a loud voice to all the birds in my backyard. I want to dance naked in my bathroom to the polka, and I don't even close the curtains. We have stored our firewood in anticipation of using it in our wood-burning stove. The canning of fruit and vegetables is finished and stored in the pantry. Now is the time to gather and prepare for winter. We are holding our notes longer during this two-four time.

The winter of our lives is bringing us to a close. It's the season when there are more years behind us than before us. None of us know the exact date when our hearts will expire and we take our last breath on this planet. Given that reality, we should try a little harder to capture the moments we've been given. Capturing the moment means that we'll do things like love more deeply, forgive more quickly, listen more carefully, and speak more affirmingly. Winter is the season when we stay in, warm our feet by the fire, read books, visit with loved ones, and gaze out the window to view God's way of decorating.

God's Decorating

Winter is also a time for celebration. I love Christmas. I think it's good to have Christmas in the middle of winter. It's a good time to celebrate the birthday of Jesus. We're not sure of the exact date of His birth. However, just when the frost is heavy in the air and some hearts are equally as heavy and tired of struggling, along comes a birthday party. It's a time to celebrate.

Several years ago, during a service on Christmas Eve, I watched the choir assemble in front of the congregation while the director took his place on the stage and the pianist her place at the piano. She began to play, and the singers launched into a well-known Christian song that started with these words by Brian Doerksen: "Come, now is the time to worship." I was surprised. I expected "Silent Night," written by Franz Xaver Gruber and Joseph Mohr, or some other time-honored Christmas carol. The song I heard was appropriate. It should be a time to worship.

All life must die; it's the way of things. Just like the flower bulbs that rest throughout the winter in frozen soil, seemingly dead, we rest throughout life and look forward to a rebirth. We anticipate the warmth of spring and the splendor of a new life. There is more to life than just the four seasons of a year. We spend time in each one as we travel toward the unknown. I have always thought that there has to be something more after winter. *Why else would we spend our whole lives learning and growing,* I would think, *not just to fade away into nothing?* I sing praises to my Father in heaven, praises of his wonderfulness and mercy. Because in the spring of our lives, the Son fills us with His warmth and we gather all we can throughout the summer, allowing us to store that warmth in autumn, so we may draw upon it for strength in the winter when it becomes necessary.

There is no simple, single time signature for the winter of our lives. All times are gathered together for one song. The song of a life well spent.

My song of praise: "In Moments Like These" by David Graham.
Bible quote: (Ephesians 1:3 NAS) "Blessed be the God and Father of our Lord Jesus Christ, who has blessed us with every spiritual blessing in the heavenly places in Christ."

CHAPTER 11

Key Signature

Every piece of music has a key signature. In musical notation, a key signature is a series of flat or sharp symbols placed on the staff to designate notes that are to be consistently played one-half step higher or lower than the equivalent natural notes, unless otherwise altered with an accidental. Key signatures are generally written immediately after the clef at the beginning of a line of musical notation. All this information may help the musician to play a song correctly, but what about the vocalist?

One of the biggest complaints from our instrument-playing friends is that we singers rarely know in which key their music is to be performed. In fact, I asked a couple of my vocalist friends what their key preference was, and they responded with a quizzical, "I don't know." I wonder how they can ask an accompanist to play a song for them and know that they would be able to sing it successfully. No voice is exactly the same. That's why songs are written in many different keys. What about me? I didn't know what key would best suit my vocal ability. I found out though, in a most interesting way.

A few summers ago, I was asked by a professional musician by the name of Max (not his real name) to sing at a ragtime music festival in the city of Shaniko, Oregon. I love to sing, so I was immediately interested; however, I was not familiar with the city of Shaniko, so I looked it up on the Internet.

Shaniko is located in central Oregon. It was known as the "Wool Capital of the World" during the first decade of the twentieth century and the hub of the Columbia Southern Railway, a subsidary of Union Pacific Railroad. The railroad provided service for a twenty-thousand-square-mile area for the transportation of such products as wool, wheat, cattle, and sheep. By 1911, because the rail system was diverted around the town, Shaniko began to decline. A mid-1960s flood in Hay Canyon near Grass Valley destroyed part of the Columbia Southern line and led to its abandonment. As of the census of 2000, there were twenty-six people—fourteen households and nine families—residing within the city. It is considered a virtual ghost town. I couldn't wait to visit this little city, if I could indeed find it.

My first question to Max after I learned a little bit about the city was whether or not there were running water and electricity. His answer was, "Sort of!" I thought, *What kind of an answer is that?* The distance between my home in Glendale and Shaniko is 290 miles, which is a five-and-a-half-hour drive. I was a little apprehensive when I talked to Max, but he assured me that it would be fun, adding that he would pay me one hundred dollars for the gig. How could I refuse?

I told Max I would think about it. I knew that my friend Meleani was due to travel up from Twain Harte, California, for a visit, so I gave her a call and asked her about traveling with me to Shaniko. I knew she loved to travel. I didn't tell her about the maybe electricity and running water situation or the fact that twenty-six people lived there. I told her how far it was in distance and time and asked if she'd like go with me. Her answer was an excited, "Let's do it." She planned to arrive on the Wednesday before the weekend of the festival. We would head for Shaniko on Friday.

Meleani was not familiar with ragtime music. She is an accomplished opera singer and on occasion sings in various California opera choruses. She also sings Christian music. I sing Christian and popular music. We both love music and really love an adventure. Mel and I have shared many adventures from church retreats to community choirs. We lived in the same city in California for many years, went to the same church, and even sang in the same choir. The choir is where I met her. She has been my friend for over fifteen years. When my husband and I retired to Oregon, she and her husband moved even farther away to a home among the mountains of California. Her trip to my house would take her close to nine hours. Heading to Shaniko would take another six hours. We were both excited to be a part of a ragtime festival. At best, I was promised a nice hotel room at the local hotel that had been refurbished. At the very least, I would have a cot at the home of one of Shaniko's residents. Mel and I decided to pack a couple of sleeping bags and air mattresses, just in case we needed them.

After many hours of driving, we finally arrived in Shaniko, travel weary and very hungry. We found the hotel where Max suggested we stay and also found the sign in the front door window. It said, "Closed." That was strike one in a game I wasn't all that comfortable playing. We drove around the block and found an ice-cream parlor. The lights were out and there was a sign in its door. It said, "Closed at 5:00 P.M." I looked at my watch, which showed the time was 5:15. Strike two! Did I mention we were very hungry? Both of us felt discouraged and a little grumpy. I suggested we go back to the gas station at the edge of town, fill up the tank, and perhaps purchase some chips and soda. After that, we would search for Max.

To our amazement, we realized that the gas station was also the local diner. We entered the red and yellow building, spotted a table at the corner by the window, and plunked our tired bodies down. It was enjoyable just to be out of the car.

We decided on a couple of sandwiches and a soda. The waitress, who also was the owner of the diner, filled us in on much of the city gossip, especially about the battle between the city council and the hotel owners, ultimately leading to the closure of the hotel. A lot of people lost their jobs. My thoughts went back to what I had found out about the town population being twenty-six and wondered where all the employees came from and where they went. We ate what we could of our meal and asked for a take-out box. We found out a lot about the small city, much of which we promptly forgot.

We were to meet Max at the old schoolhouse on Turner Avenue. I didn't have a map, so we just drove around looking for what we imagined a turn-of-the-century one-room schoolhouse would look like. We imagined the type of schoolhouse you see in all the old western movies. You know, the little red building with a bell hanging by the front door. As we drove around Shaniko, we realized that it was divided in half by one large highway slithering through the business district with an S curve eventually heading to Bend, Oregon. At least, that's what the blue sign indicated with an arrow pointing north.

As we entered the S curve, my attention was focused on the search for a red schoolhouse. I was looking to the right when I heard Mel shout, "There it is! Over there to the left." I looked to the left and started to apply the brakes in anticipation of a turn. I glanced in my rear-view mirror and noticed a tractor-trailer bearing down on my bumper, so I decided to make a sharp turn to get out of the way. That's when I saw another tractor-trailer truck coming at me from the other direction. In a split-second decision, I tromped on the gas and turned right in front of the large, silver bulldog glued to the hood of the truck aimed at my windshield. When I think back on that indiscretion, I see my car flying off the road and landing on Turner Avenue. Of course, that's not what happened. It actually was a few seconds of panic with screeching tires and stones and dust flying everywhere.

"Well!" I huffed to my speechless friend who had a death grip on the dash. "That was pretty tricky." We realized that evening as we headed toward the center of town that crossing the S curve by foot was just as much a challenge as with a vehicle. I pulled into the parking space in front of the old schoolhouse and stared at the bright green building with the large wooden doors.

"Mel," I said as I turned the motor off, "how did you know that this was the schoolhouse? It's green, not red."

"I saw the huge bell tower on the roof."

I looked up to the roof, and sure enough, there was a large bell in what looked like a big doghouse. There was nothing more I could say to my friend except that I was sorry for almost killing her.

Although we were both shocked by the bright green building, not a red building as we had imagined, we were satisfied that this was indeed the meeting place. We grabbed our bags and headed for the dirt path that led to the double doors. We walked through the doorway and stepped into a time warp. To the right, there was a small room filled with handmade offerings for sale, and to the left was a large room that smelled of old books and chalk. As we turned to the left and headed for the large schoolroom, we promised each other that tomorrow we would pay a visit to the little gift shop.

I heard the *plunk, plunk* of piano keys as we entered the large schoolroom. Max was elbow deep inside an old upright piano, tuning it for the next day's performance. He looked up with a grin and a friendly hello. I greeted him in a not so friendly way and got right to the point about our lodging and the apparent lack of it. I asked about the hotel that was closed. I also asked where we were going to stay. He told us he was sorry and that he had found out about the hotel closure when he arrived. He asked if we brought along sleeping bags as he pointed to the stage area, explaining further that we could sleep up there. He also told us that there was a bathroom down the hall. I asked about his friend's house and the cots that were supposed to be available, only to hear an apology and see the glance toward one single cot that he had secured to use himself but would be willing to give up for one of us. Definitely, a strike three!

I looked at Mel; she stared back in shock. I knew she wasn't pleased. I wasn't exactly comfortable with the situation. There was nothing we could do but unload the car. We brought our suitcases in and set them on the stage. After a couple of trips back and forth to the car, we finally set the rest of our bedding on the stage and decided to check out the bathroom. The whole situation got a little worse, if that was even possible. There was no shower or bathtub, only a toilet, a sink, and a mirror. And no electric plugs!

"We can't stay here, Di. I can't use that bathroom with no plugs. How will I curl my hair?"

I didn't argue with Mel. Quite frankly, I didn't know what to say. I reassured her that everything would be okay, but I knew she was ready to leave and find a motel that, I might add, was at least forty-five miles north. Max must have seen the shocked look on our faces, because he explained that there was an extension cord we could use. He pointed to two huge, fifteen-foot-high folding doors on each side of the room and said, "These folding doors will close to give you privacy." He also explained that he had a friend in town that might let us take a shower.

Really? I knew that would never happen.

So there we were, two city gals stuck in a virtual ghost town with minimal modern conveniences. I pointed out to Mel that at least we had flush toilets, never mind that the flow of water from the sink tap hesitated and the lights dimmed when the handle went down. I actually thought it was pretty funny. My friend did not. We just stood there in disbelief, in the middle of the stage that would convert into our bedroom. I was sure it couldn't get much worse.

In between loud notes being played and adjusted on the piano, Max shouted out the weekend program schedule. I stood there listening, and suddenly, my mind flashed back fifty years to that country house and the old upright piano of my childhood that sat in the backroom. I saw the young girl elbow deep in tuning that piano with a skate key.

Max picked up his tool-kit and rushed to the front door, yelling over his shoulder that he had two more pianos to tune and "Oh, by the way, the first jam session is at seven thirty tonight at the Old Sage Saloon and Trading Post!" He turned to me as he opened the door to leave and with a flip of his hand announced that we could practice later. The door slammed shut. We were alone.

I'm not sure how long we stood there in silence wondering what had just happened. We eventually walked to the edge of the stage, sat down with our legs dangling, looked at each other, and howled with laughter until we gasped for breath. We knew that complaining would be useless. Resigned to the crazy weekend we were about to encounter, we shrugged our shoulders, helped each other up, and proceeded to get our bedding ready. "Thank you, Lord," was our only response. "Thank you that we decided to include air mattresses and sleeping bags." I even had an electric air pump.

As the time approached seven o'clock, we decided to head for the saloon, wherever that was. The only scary thought was crossing the S curve. As it turned out, the whole city was like an old western movie set where an outlaw could be seen walking down Main Street, gun in hand and spurs dinging the dirt as he prepared to shoot his way out of town.

The music had already started, so we were successful in finding our first concert location. We entered the room through swinging saloon doors and walked into the 1800s. The upright piano rested against the wall. I couldn't believe my eyes when I spotted the old twirly-top stool that supported Max with his white sleeves held up by garters and his red satin vest. The room was filled with the music of "Ragtime Suzie." People were sitting and standing at the old-time bar. There were metal folding chairs set up in a few rows facing the piano. I counted about twenty as Mel and I headed for a couple of seats in the back row.

Max had his own band, including another piano player, a saxophonist, and a trumpeter. I leaned toward Mel and whispered that I had my two harmonicas in my pocket. She looked at me sternly and threatened me with bodily harm if I even put my hand near my pocket. I couldn't help but notice that she was a little edgy. I had no clue as to what I was supposed to do, so I just sat down and tried to hide under my friend. As it turned out, I did sing a few songs. It's just that my expectations were somewhat different from the actual performance. I was a little uncomfortable. I'm just thankful that my friend stuck it out with me and didn't hate me forever.

After the evening's music session, we headed back to our sleeping quarters on the stage in a one-room schoolhouse that really had two or even three rooms. It only seemed right that Mel and I share a stage, being the two performers that we were. I just didn't think it would be in sleeping bags.

Max arrived shortly after we did, asking if it would be okay to practice tomorrow afternoon instead of the morning. He explained that he had to make a couple of deliveries to some people in town after breakfast. That was okay with me. He groaned as he knelt to retrieve his suitcase that rested under the only cot in the room, expressing as he pulled it out that he was really tired. I was tired too. I just wanted to go to bed. Mel and I looked at each other with the same thought as Max pawed through his clothes and pulled out striped pajamas. Was he going to get into his PJs right in front of us? Finally, I spoke up and suggested we close the giant doors. We struggled with the very tall wooden room dividers and after a lot of pushing and pulling succeeded in securing some privacy.

The day ended with Mel and me snug in our sleeping bags, on a stage in an old schoolhouse. As I closed my eyes, I heard Mel whisper, "I hope he doesn't snore."

Morning arrived and we both just hid in our sleeping bags while wondering how the heck we were going to get out of bed, get to the bathroom, and get dressed without anyone seeing us. As it turned out, there was no one around, not even Max. I decided to get up first because I didn't require a lot of fussing. I threw on my blue jeans and sweatshirt, washed my face and combed my hair, and finished several other necessities, taking only thirty minutes. So I was surprised to see that Mel had gotten up, let the air out of the mattresses, and rolled up the sleeping bags. I helped her get the extension cord set up so she could do her hair and makeup. I thought it went rather smoothly. While Mel was in the bathroom, I brewed some coffee in the two-cup coffee maker I remembered to bring. All in all, I was pretty content with our progress, thinking morning wasn't too difficult. At least, I don't remember it being difficult. Now Mel might have another story to tell. Because she is my true best friend, not one complaint came out of her throughout the whole weekend, just those unbelievable looks every once in a while.

After we finished our breakfast at the local diner/gas station, we took a tour through the town square, stopping at a few gift shops along the way. It was truly an old ghost town with history hanging around all the old buildings. We found a jail and took turns behind the bars. There was the warehouse full of very old, rusty, dusty cars and wagons. An old horse-drawn fire truck rested in the park. After a few hours, we arrived at the ice-cream parlor. Who can pass up ice cream? The poster on the front door told of a free spaghetti dinner with Christian music in the town of Antelope. Luckily, it was the same day, so we asked for directions. The waitress responded, "It's just down the road. You can't miss it." We decided that we would have time to go there and come back for the evening show if we left right after the afternoon practice with Max.

Shaniko

When we arrived back at the schoolhouse for the afternoon practice, Max was there and ready. He thanked me for waiting until the afternoon to practice. He was able to deliver all the CDs of his piano playing to a couple of his wife's friends. After assuring him that all was fine and after we told him of our tour of the town, Mel pulled out her book to read and I gave him the music I had brought. We picked out some songs he would play while I sang. The first question he asked me was what key

I wanted him to play. *What key?* I didn't have a clue as to what my key of preference was when singing. But there was the question.

I firmly believe that in every situation, whether good or bad, there is something to learn. That afternoon, I learned my comfortable vocal key signature. It is B flat. We practiced all my songs in that key. The sound of my singing would be in the middle, not too high and not too low. After an hour of practice, we were satisfied with the plans we made for the evening's performance. Max was off to what he called a jam session with the girls.

Mel and I decided to head for Antelope with the hope we would actually find the little city. We had plenty of time to get there, eat, and be back by the eight-thirty show. After traveling eight miles of descending S curves, on what seemed like a single-lane road, we arrived at Antelope and found the local diner that was hosting the spaghetti dinner. This city was actually smaller than Shaniko. The tables were set on an adjoining lawn facing a stage that would hold the Christian singing group. We sat at a table covered with a plastic red-and-white checkered tablecloth, ate great spaghetti with meatballs, and listened to very familiar Christian music. We had a wonderful time. We were a little afraid of traveling back on the winding road in the dark, so we left right after we ate.

Cars were already parked in front of the schoolhouse when we arrived. Some people were inside the little gift shop and others were taking their seats for the show. I felt the excitement in the air as I headed to our stage bedroom to change into my clothes for the performance. After I was dressed, I peeked through the wooden folding doors to watch the unused classroom fill up with people eager to hear the ragtime music. The doors were closed at the back of the room as Max stood to introduce himself. The audience responded to him with affection as he took his seat at the piano and began the performance. He played several ragtime selections. The trumpeter filled in with a couple of songs, and the saxophonist played the biggest saxophone I had ever seen. The whole gang was very talented.

Finally, it was my turn. I don't mind admitting that I was just a little nervous. I was to enter the room from behind the folding doors while wearing an old-time outfit that looked like I had stepped off a stage in an old saloon. Mel was in the audience with her camcorder ready to film my debut as a paid performer.

The first song began, and to my horror, Max was playing the song in the wrong key, almost but not quite out of my range. I gave him a shocked "What the heck are you playing?" look that I'm sure communicated my confusion in the fact that he was playing in the wrong key. Too late. He smiled and kept right on playing; there was no turning back. I thought, *So much for rehearsal and knowing what my best key is.* The audience never had a clue what was happening, as evidenced by their applause.

Life is very much like that performance. There always seems to be a period of adjustment, a time that requires change with only a few seconds notice and a time when we must pull from our experience to proceed.

The best part of the weekend was the totally surprised look on Max's face when he asked if anyone would like to present a song and I pointed to Mel. I introduced Mel to the guest piano player and gave her the music to "Climb Every Mountain" by Ernest Lehman. Mel sang the song perfectly and brought the house down. You see, she is a professional opera singer. What a thrill for me to see her perform. I'm sure it made the whole trip better for her as she listened to the applause.

My Friend, Mel

Sunday morning arrived and we had a small church service with more beautiful music—my favorite music: Christian music. I think it was the best presentation of the whole weekend. After the service, knowing we had a lot of miles to drive, we packed up, thanked everyone, and headed out the door for home. Our adventure to the small city of Shaniko was over. It had been a fun time for both of us after all. And the most important part of the whole trip was I learned my own special key and I didn't let the fact that it was B flat affect my confidence in singing.

My song of praise: "The Steadfast Love of the Lord Never Ceases" by Robert Davidson.
Bible quote: (Philippians 4:7 NAS) "And the peace of God, which surpasses all comprehension, shall guard your hearts and your minds in Christ Jesus."

CHAPTER 12

Voice

A voice type is a particular kind of human singing voice perceived as having certain identifying qualities. Voice classification is the process by which human voices are evaluated and thereby designated into voice types. These qualities include but are not limited to vocal range, vocal weight, vocal tessitura, vocal timbre, and vocal transition points, such as breaks and lifts within the voice. I recently learned of two systems that differentiate voice types. One originated in Europe and is called the German Fach System. It's used in opera. The other is used in America and is called the choral music system. There is no system universally applied or accepted.

Within a choir are six types of voices: soprano (the highest female voice), mezzo-soprano (a female voice in between the soprano and alto), alto (the lowest female voice), tenor (the highest male voice), baritone (a male voice in between the tenor and bass), and bass (the lowest male voice). Interestingly, some men can sing in the same range as women by using their falsetto voice.

The voice has personality. Heartache or joy can be heard in a song as it is sung. You might be thinking that of course you know it's a song about hurt or joy. Just listen to the words. Ah, but it's not just the words of a song. It's the way it's delivered. Certain voice inflections can cause an audience to weep as they listen to a song. What about fast pace—happy songs with happy words? That type of song most often will urge people to clap their hands and smile. However, if the performer sings with a slow rhythm with certain pauses, it can be happy words sung sadly. A flat note in a song seems to evoke sad feelings, whereas a sharp note lifts the song to a more positive feeling.

A voice is an important element to understand, not just in singing a song but in communication. Not everyone can sing, but everyone has a voice. We have a voice in all we do. For me, in an uncomfortable situation, my voice is one of comedy. For a person who just can't seem to relax and have fun, his or her voice may be one of work. Sometimes a voice, especially when singing, is not realized as a gift but taken for granted and used as just another task. The enjoyment is missing and the blessing is lost.

Can a person's voice really tell you about the person inside? Does a person's voice say happy or sad or black or white? Does it tell you about their self-esteem and if they are a nice person or not? Can a person's voice clue you as to whether or not that individual is good-hearted?

So what's in a voice? Everything! I think if you really listen to people speak, you can tell everything. I believe you can tell if they are hurting inside, if they are happy, if they are telling the truth or not, and just how much goodness is deep down in their hearts. The key is in the voice, and the key is to listen.

Whether you speak slowly or quickly, loudly or softly, in a deep voice or a high-pitched voice, pause (or don't pause) between sentences, all of it says something about the person you are inside. Changing your speaking habits can prove to be a difficult task, even impossible. Ultimately, the person inside will always seep out no matter what disguise is used.

Individually a voice well spoken can change history. One great struggle is the voice that women fought for during the suffrage movement starting in 1848 and continuing until 1920. Even today women struggle for a voice. Today, we take it for granted that women can vote, but there was a time when they could not. Can you imagine?

Throughout history we have been introduced to many famous voices. Mark Twain's voice spoke in his writing. Helen Keller's voice started with hand movements and evolved into speaking on women's rights. John the Baptist used his voice to introduce the Savior. He was described as "a voice crying in the desert."

As a child, I was raised in an atmosphere of total control. I had no voice in any activity or family function. I developed my own voice as I grew and matured. I found music as my voice. It is the key to all that I believe in. When I was eight years old, Grandmother Rie taught me to sing her favorite song, titled "Little Things Mean a Lot" by Edith Lindeman and Carl Stutz. I can remember sitting on the arm of her overstuffed chair and repeating each phrase as she sang it to me, until I could sing it alone. It was the most beautiful song I had ever heard, and it has followed me throughout my life. During the last fifty years, I have heard it presented in many different arrangements. Even today as I write this chapter, I hear it playing on the radio.

I had the opportunity to speak at a women's luncheon last summer for a church in our area. The theme of the luncheon was "little things matter." I knew that I had to sing that song. What a thrill, after fifty years, to be able to sing a song I had first learned when I was eight. I can just imagine Grandmother Rie saying to everyone in heaven, "Hush, that's my granddaughter singing. I taught her that song." The ladies at the luncheon loved it.

Not everyone can sing, but every person has a voice. My voice is to tell the story about my God. It is of Thee I sing. Let your voice be heard. Please, don't die with the music in you.

My song of praise: "I Love You, Lord, and I Lift My Voice" by Laurie Klein.

Bible quote: (Isaiah 28:23 NAS) "Give ear and hear my voice. Listen and hear my words."

SECTION 5

Acceptance

CHAPTER 13

The Medleys of Life

As I stand at my kitchen window and gaze out across the backyard, I wonder at the many colors of nature, and I'm amazed at God's gardening. The tall, dark-green pines stand over small, light-green shrubs with red berries while a smattering of flowers left from summer plantings add yellow and white to the lawn. On the patio, my geraniums splash their red and pink blooms, inviting the dance of the hummingbirds looking for nectar. However, the hanging bottle feeder eventually lures them to rest and drink its sweet liquid. There is harmony throughout my yard. The tiny birds flit from one bush to another, tasting leftover berries. The bossy blue jays attack the feeder hanging on the back porch, spilling seeds everywhere. It's an entertaining scene that gives me a relaxed moment as I rinse off a few dishes in the sink after breakfast. The tallest pine tree catches my eye as the first morning rays of the rising sun splash

tall pines

against its branches. The very peak of the tree shimmers and flutters as small birds fight for position, eventually resting to bask in the warmth of the sun. The whole scene is a medley of colors, textures, and activity.

In music, an arrangement of various melodies is called a medley. I was introduced to the concept of a medley at a Christian retreat I attended with my friend Meleani. We wanted to sing a song together and decided on "In the Garden Medley," an arrangement by Sandy Patty. I was a little nervous, having never sung with her, but she reassured me and taught me what to sing, and it turned out great. It was three songs in one: "In the Garden" by Charles Austin Miles, "What a Friend We Have in Jesus" by Joseph M. Scriven, and "Just a Closer Walk with Thee" by unknown. I think fondly of my friend and the times we spent together as I take in the scene of my backyard and my beautiful garden medley.

The beautiful plant life in a backyard, a sunset over a mountain range, or a garden full of flowers can be very relaxing and comforting to view. We need only to see what is before us, not just with our eyes but with our hearts. Our subconscious constantly takes pictures of what habitually passes before our eyes and stores the information in our brains as memory. Our internal cameras snap away as we drive by a church, a school, a lake, or even road signs along the journey back and forth to work every day. Eventually, our brain accesses what I call "pictures of recognition" and gives us a familiar feeling of contentment rather than a confusing, lost panic attack.

When I first moved to California and tried to drive throughout the city where we lived, I felt constant panic and confusion. I would run stop signs, turn in the wrong direction from the wrong street lane, and even run over curbs. My ten-year-old son began to wonder about my driving ability. Confusion ensued for a couple of months, until my subconscious had gathered all the familiar scenes that passed by my eyes. Finally, I no longer felt uncomfortable. Of course, I no longer noticed the landmarks I drove by either. My mind recorded everything without my even noticing. Oftentimes, we take for granted all the beauty that surrounds us as we travel through life. We see so many sunsets that we don't notice the beautiful oranges and reds that stripe the sky. Snow gathers on the top of mountains and melts and gathers again in silence as we go about our daily routines.

Medleys appear in life as situations occurring because of decisions. The paths we take lead us to the lives we currently have. I have always based my decisions on emotion and availability. Did it feel right and was it attainable? I graduated from high school during a time when getting married and raising a family was the norm. It seemed my right decision at the time. I created my own medley: a husband, babies, a home, and a wish to live happily ever after. The first marriage didn't work out, but I have no regrets with my choice. I moved on and created another medley.

Choices may make our lives interesting and entertaining, but what about the lives that are affected without a choice being made? I remember my brother-in-law Bill, who committed suicide and left his family distraught with unanswered questions as to why he would do such a thing. The family didn't choose this to happen, yet it changed the direction of their lives. Sickness can descend on a family, killing a young child after thousands of dollars in medical bills. The family did not choose this direction, yet they had to make the trip.

When my current husband and I moved to Modesto, California, we lived in what I think of as a medley of nine different homes in twenty years, not always by choice. We held many positions of employment—again, not always by choice. I adjusted until I found the right position for me. My husband retired and decided that Modesto was not the city where he wanted us to live out our years. Another move? Here we go again. I was settled in a good job, going to a great church, singing in a wonderful choir, and enjoying my daughter and grandchildren. Why on earth would I want to give that up and move to another state?

I'm sure you've heard of the title of Shakespeare's play *The Comedy of Errors*. Our life, after the decision to move, became a *medley* of errors. Everything had to be done in a certain order to facilitate retiring, selling one house, purchasing another house, and finding another job in order to leave my present one. The biggest question: where would we live? While we prepared to sell the house in California, we searched the Internet to find a house in Oregon. I was also looking for another place to work. There are times when I felt like I was getting tossed in a giant bowl of greens. You know, the packages of many types of lettuce called "salad medley" that hang on a hook in the produce department of a grocery store.

My husband and I spent a lot of time looking through real estate brochures only to find that time after time, the house we were interested in was already sold. I made a trip with my friend Meleani to scope out the Oregon area. We drove north on Interstate 5 to Portland and then over to the coastal highway. As I was becoming familiar with the state I was to reside in, I fell in love with Oregon. It had two things close to my heart: mountains and evergreen trees. But where on earth would I find a home to live in?

Mel and I would look for signs that indicated that a house was being offered for sale. One place we intended to visit was up a very steep, long driveway. We were in a minivan, and Mel was driving—*fearfully,* I might add. As we traveled up the driveway, it actually felt like the front end of the car was going to pop up and we would somersault backward. Mel stated quite seriously that she was going to turn around. "I can't get up this hill, Di. We are going to tip over." I agreed with her and was happy when we headed back down the driveway. Some houses just weren't meant to be seen and are not worth the stress of getting to them. Later that year, my husband and I found the same property, and he just flew up the steep driveway. He was a lot braver than Mel or I.

Our plans all came together, but not without error. After two years of work, the house in California never sold, and we ended up losing it. We purchased a house close to an interstate so if I had to drive miles to work, I would be near the main highway. My husband retired and moved to the house in Oregon, while I continued to work in California. We were separated for close to a year until I found employment.

I wasn't happy with having to quit a job I loved to move to a strange state and start over. But God knew what was going to happen so I relied on my faith to guide me. I hated the new job, but it paid the bills for as long as we needed. We found a church and yes, I found another choir.

In my life, I've had many medleys that have taught me serious lessons. When your life becomes a series of medleys, good or bad, strength is created that enables the ability to cope. I loved my husband; therefore, I would go wherever he wanted to go. He thought Oregon would be enjoyable and safe. I gave up a great deal to move to California to be with my husband, and now I was to give up a great deal more. Did I pray about it? You bet! I know, you're thinking that finally this woman has prayed about her direction in life. I have learned the hard way that God has a way to direct believers to where they can be used to glorify Him. God was directing me north. I had a peace about the move and felt that I was doing the right thing.

I remember a statement that my first husband made after several years of marriage. He told me that someday he would like to move to Oregon. Perhaps God wanted me there even thirty years ago. There again are the turns to the left or the right and the choices we make creating medleys of life.

Knowing that there is someone tracking my travels and watching my every step sometimes brings fear to my heart, fear that I will be willful and take the wrong turn. As a Christian, it also brings great joy and assurance. God's hand is in my life, and He leads me in every direction; I've only to listen to the medley He plays in my heart.

My story doesn't end here. There's a lesson I learned about a deep hurt that I had harbored for many years. You see, more than anything, I wanted to sing. I wanted to sing solos with my church choir. I kept that hurt buried for so long that I forgot it was there. I had hundreds of songs that I knew, with no place to sing. I left a church in Modesto because the director would not ask me to sing. I attended another church and was allowed to sing solos, only to find that we were leaving California to live in Oregon. Were there churches in Oregon?

Our new house was in the woods in the mountains near a couple of small towns that were called "cities." What was God thinking? This was a new medley for me. There is a term in music one uses to describe a chord progression that seems to lead to resolving itself on the final chord but does not. The term is *deceptive cadence*. It kind of leaves you hanging. I couldn't help but wonder if this move would be the final move to no place, a place where I could no longer sing because there would be no place to sing.

Our house was at least thirty-five miles from any major city. There were no nursing homes to visit. I didn't know of any churches like the ones I liked in California. Dave was attending a Saturday night service in Glendale at a Presbyterian church. I'm not a Presbyterian. I had no church and no place to sing. Perhaps this was a hanging medley with no resolve.

I named this situation "the Olivet Medley." Olivet is the little church in Glendale that my husband picked out because of a man he'd met. The man died, but we got to know his wife. She had a son who was leaving a bad marriage. My daughter visited us from California, met the son, and they fell in love and eventually got married. My daughter was happy. My friend's son was happy. As it turned out, Olivet Church had a small choir consisting of half the congregation. I needed to sing, so I asked if I could join the choir. "What do you sing?" the choir director asked. Ah, there's the question I'm used to hearing. "I'm an alto," I replied.

Every once in a while, I run across a poem that tells a story and solves a dilemma. I think that poems are a beautiful way to express one's thoughts. I wanted to share this one with you.

Dianne Coon

The Loom of Time
Author Unknown

Man's life is laid in the loom of time
To a pattern he does not see,
While the weaver works and the shuttles fly,
Till the dawn of eternity.

Some shuttles are filled with silver thread
And some with threads of gold,
While often but the darker hue
Is all that they may hold.

But the weaver watches with skillful eye
Each shuttle fly to and fro
And sees the pattern so deftly wrought
As the loom moves sure and slow.

God surely planned the pattern ...
Each thread the dark and fair,
Is chosen by his master skill
And placed in the web with care.

He, only, knows its beauty
And guides the shuttles which hold
The threads so unattractive,
As well as the threads of gold.

Not till each loom is silent
And their shuttles cease to fly

Shall God unroll the pattern
And explain the reason why.

The dark threads were as needful
In the weaver's skillful hand
As the threads of gold and silver
For the pattern which He has planned.

So what was the lesson I learned? Everything in life, good or bad, asked for or not, is directed by God. Every medley occurring has an end. My favorite song to sing at my church is "In the Garden Medley." The very first medley I learned. I am where God wanted me all along. He rewarded my obedience with a wonderful husband for my daughter, a wonderful choir for me to sing in, and a church with a great pastor.

My song of praise: "Through It All" by Andrae Crouch.
Bible quote: (Isaiah 58:11 NAS) "The Lord will guide you continually."

CHAPTER 14

A Cappella

I've discussed orchestras; all kinds of music; all types of sound; learning to sing with accompany tapes and now CDs; and learning to sing with other singers in a choir, a small group, or a trio. What about singing alone, a single voice that begins a song with only the sound of one note usually played by a pitch pipe or a piano? The musical phrase *a cappella* is Italian for "in the manner of the church." It means to sing without instrumental sound. A group of voices singing with only each other to hear for support creates a beautiful sound.

In high school, I sang in a choir that traveled to different colleges for competition, receiving marks for presentation. In my senior year, we went to Syracuse University's School of Music to participate in a festival of music. Schools from all over Central New York were there. Each choir would sing three songs: two with the piano and one a cappella. The a cappella song Mrs. Downer, our director, chose was "Ave Maria." This arrangement had an introductory solo that was given to me. It was my task to sing the first line using only a pitch pipe to begin.

The sixty-voice choir stood on risers in a huge auditorium with me on the top riser in the alto section. Mrs. Downer picked up her pitch pipe and played the note I was to start on, a "G" above middle "C." I was completely alone, just me and the sound of a "G" from a pitch pipe floating through the air. I sang. The choir joined in at exactly the right time, and we finished. We received an "A" and wonderful remarks. The image of that sixteen-year-old girl standing on the top riser in the alto section of the choir is clear in my memory.

There were many times in my life when I felt completely alone, sometimes even in the midst of a crowd. I felt alone in the love I had for three men, alone in childbirth and the joy of raising three children, alone with the death of my parents, alone in my sickness, and alone with my husband's sickness. Most of the time, feeling alone gave me a hurtful feeling, a lonely feeling, not that there was no one to turn to but the feeling that no one really understood or cared. One time in my old church in Modesto, after church finished, I was leaving the choir room when I met a fellow choir member at the door. She said, "Hello. How are you?" I paused and answered, "Hi, I'm not feeling well today." Those words hung in the air as she hurried on without a second's hesitation. She didn't really care how I felt.

Alone is entirely internal. When I picked up my divorce papers ending the marriage to my first husband, I left the attorney's office, stood by my car, folded the papers, and stuffed them in my purse. I got in the car and headed home. I was alone. This was an a cappella moment with no instrumental music accompaniment to my crying.

The faith and love I have for my Lord Jesus Christ is an internal feeling, and I am alone in it. A cappella, without help, is how my soul lifts praise to Thee, my God. I found it easy to praise God when my life was in a state of peace. This was not the case at the beginning of January 2013, when the peace in my life was eliminated.

I stood in the hall looking into a glassed room at a hospital bed that contained my husband. I just stared at him lying in the bed with needles in his arm, clothes off and discarded to a chair. He was already dressed in a white gown with nurses and doctors hovering over him. Only his eyes moved to meet mine—eyes full of fear. I felt like a child needing a hand to hold. I was alone. Two men dressed in white entered the room and started to wheel the bed out. My eyes connected again with my husband's. He knew I was there. "Where are you taking him?" I asked.

I was directed to a chair alongside one of the glassed walls and asked to please sit. "We're taking him to X-ray," was the answer.

With helpless resign, I sat down. It had only been one half hour since leaving the restaurant. In that one-half hour, my life changed. My best friend in the world, the love of my life, my husband was in mortal trouble. I was alone and afraid with at least a hundred questions. However, I had to wait in the glassed room, clutching my purse fighting back tears.

As I waited, I pondered the last hour's events, wondering what I could have done differently. It never occurred to me to call an ambulance from the restaurant. I knew as we sat waiting for our meal that something was wrong. My husband was having difficulty reading the menu; he couldn't hold his fork, and he was staring over my shoulder. I asked him what he was looking at, and his response was, "The woman I love." I thought that remark to be odd. Not that this was the only time he ever said he loved me, but because of the far-away look in his eyes and the sound of his voice. I ordered shrimp for him and a salad for me. The shrimp in the large bowl that arrived all had tails on them, tails that my husband could not get off. He searched his food for carrots that weren't there and asked for peaches. The whole situation was bizarre, and I was beginning to get really nervous. I ate fast and helped him best I could. Somehow, I felt that time was of the essence. We needed to finish our meals, and I needed to get him to a hospital.

After he finished his meal, I asked for the check and paid the bill, all the while watching my husband slump in his chair. I helped him with his coat and guided him toward the stairs that led to the door. I placed his right arm over my neck and held his hand with my right hand while wrapping my left hand around his belt, practically carrying him down the two flights of stairs. We headed up the boardwalk to the path that led to our car, taking rest stops along the way. He was barely able to walk. With each passing minute, I became more and more afraid and unsure what to do. I only knew that I had to take care of my husband. I knew that we had to leave and get to a hospital. The challenge I faced was where to find a veterans hospital. We were in Monterey, California, leaving a restaurant on the boardwalk. I did not know where to go.

I secured him in his seat and turned on the GPS to ask for the nearest hospital. I was looking for a veterans hospital. Precious time passed and the closest I could come was a veterinary clinic. Really?

I tossed the machine to the floor.

I started the car and drove to the ticket booth. As I paid for my parking, I asked where I could find the nearest veterans hospital, all while impatient drivers honked their horns for me to hurry and get out of their way. I got directions to turn right, go under a bridge, and turn left, and then I would be at the VA clinic. I followed the directions and ended up in the Coast Guard Library parking lot in front of a metal storage building. *Now what?* I thought. I prayed, "Please, God, I need your help. I don't know where to go." Time seemed to stand still for me as I watched my husband slump in his seat.

I stared out the windshield with tears of frustration filling my eyes. I didn't know what to do. That's when the Monterey Police car slowly drove from behind the shed, just as if someone had told him I was waiting for help. He talked with me, and after trying to talk to my husband, he suggested an ambulance. Within minutes, help came, as if they were waiting around the corner. My husband was placed into the ambulance. I watched the vehicle drive away with its sirens blaring and lights flashing. I was left in my car, alone. I did not feel panic. Only emptiness.

I followed the police car to the hospital parking lot and parked my car. The policeman then led me to the emergency entrance and down the hall to the emergency room. As we walked down the long hall, I felt very small, much like a child who was lost.

I was deep in my thoughts of ineffectiveness in helping my husband when the orderlies returned him to the glass cubical. I looked up to see a couple of doctors holding clipboards. The neurosurgeon explained that my husband had suffered a stroke affecting his occipital lobe, which in turn affected his speech, memory, vision, and thalamus. A lot of very large words were exchanged and mention of a very dangerous, expensive medicine by way of a shot that would stop any further damage. I talked to a lot of people, signed a lot of papers, and watched as the nurse injected my husband with the drug that would stop the stroke action. He had to be monitored for twenty-four hours. That was pretty frightening to me.

The whole incident left me totally numb and in a mind-set of disbelief. How could this be happening? We were supposed to be on vacation in California, walking on the beach and enjoying the warm sun. Dave had been pretty ill during Christmas and a couple of days after. We were staying at a beautiful home in Santa Cruz but he spent most of the time in a chair covered with a blanket. I should have realized he was sick and taken him to the hospital. It just didn't occur to me that he needed a doctor.

I stayed by his side as long as I could. I didn't want to leave, but the emergency room closed for visitors and I was handed a blanket and pillow and told I could sleep in the lounge on a couch. What a joke that was. I probably got three hours of sleep.

The next morning was filled with all kinds of tests. When I joined my husband in the morning, he was a little more alert. Then the tests began. He couldn't read and got his fruit names all mixed up when asked to identify them. He did not know where he lived. But he knew me! I didn't ask him if he knew my name. I was afraid he wouldn't remember.

I just sat in my chair and watched in disbelief, struggling not to cry or fall apart. I heard a voice that sounded familiar and looked to see who was standing in the entrance to our glass room. Standing there was the light of my life, my daughter Deb. She had driven from Modesto to Monterey to be with me, at least a two-hour drive. I was not alone anymore. She put her arms around me and I cried. She spent the day with me. Her presence gave me strength, and I will forever be grateful for her thoughtfulness.

My husband was in the hospital for three days, at which time he was given many tests, a lot of medicine, and very good care. However, he didn't talk and looked very confused. He could barely walk. Because there was a huge snowstorm predicted in Oregon, I needed to be on the road early Saturday morning. The drive would take at least eight hours, and I had to cross two sets of mountains to get home. I wanted to travel on Interstate 5 but could not remember how to get there from Monterey, so I followed the directions of my GPS and traveled up Interstate 1. Eventually, I ended up on Interstate 5, north of Sacramento. As I entered the mountain range between California and Oregon, the storm hit. Actually, it started out as rain, then sleet, then a little fog and wind and snow. I do remember asking God if there was anything else He wanted to throw at me.

I was driving a PT Cruiser with no special tires. The roads were filling up with snow and it seemed that I was the only one on the road. There were no cars, and especially no trucks. Usually Interstate 5 was full of all types of tractor-trailers. Finally, I saw the taillights of a car ahead of me. What a relief. I could follow someone. I knew if that car started to slide, I could stop. At the top of the highest mountain, with snow and sleet hitting the windshield, I cried out to God. My nerves were getting the best of me. It was dark, and I am sure the only company I had was a sick man who hadn't spoken in the last eight hours and an angel sitting on the roof of my car. At that moment, my husband, who had not said more than three words, lifted his head and asked me if I wanted him to drive. Oh how I wished I could have said, "Yes, please."

As I approached the downside of Ashland Mountain, I finally met up with the tractor-trailers. That also was quite a challenge, but I knew at the bottom were fair weather and clear roads. The trip was horrible, one that I won't soon forget. What was supposed to be a two-week vacation during the Christmas holidays turned into something I never want to repeat.

After a ten-hour drive, we arrived to a warm house. I helped Dave into his PJs and into bed after giving him his medicine. The highlight of the day was the shot of insulin I had to give him, something I had never done before. I remember apologizing to him if it hurt. He just said, "It's okay." I brought in a load of wood and started a fire, something else I had not done as a rule. I sat in my chair, picked up the throw pillow off the couch, covered my face, and wailed.

Because of the stroke, my husband was like a ten-year-old boy needing constant monitoring. He was extremely weak, unable to get up and down without assistance. His memory was damaged, he lost most of his words, and the sight in his right eye was damaged. The doctor at the hospital had told me that it would take my husband at least six months, maybe longer, to recover almost completely. I felt absolutely lost with no one to turn to. How would I be able to do all that was required? I didn't even know how to give him the shot of insulin that he would need at least three times a day. At times, I would sit in my office and think, *If I close my eyes and hold my breath, will all of this disappear?*

I was alone. Oh, my church family was a great help with food, cards, visits, and most importantly, prayers. The children called from New

York and Virginia, being too far away to do anything but worry over the phone. My daughter was the closest one, but she had responsibilities and could not come to me. They all reassured me that everything would be okay because I was a strong woman. I'm pretty strong when I have to be, but this wonderful strength only lasted a couple of hours and then I would fall apart. This event in my life was huge.

I found that my greatest strength came from God. The times I would cry for so long that my eyes were puffed almost shut, I would pray and God would lift the pain in my chest. I would tuck Dave in every night and sit by myself in the living room, covering my face with the throw pillow while I cried. I would cry until I remembered God. I would then feel the warmth of His love fill me and take away the tears.

It's been six months since my husband's stroke. I feel like this has been a test of my character and faith. My life has been full of tests, the growing-up stuff, the learning-to-get-along-with-others and the dos-and-the-don'ts-of-life tests. I was not given the gift of help by the Holy Spirit. Many times, my husband would get sick and take to his bed, and I would leave him there and hope he would get better. We both would sometimes joke about it. Sickness would scare me because I didn't know what to do. This time, I could not let him stay in his bed until he was better. I had to face what was going on and get over myself.

My husband's mental capacity has improved, and he is gaining each day. Today, he can tell me his address, something he couldn't do one month ago. I don't know if he will completely recover. That's in God's hands.

As I was sitting in church a couple of weeks ago during the confession-of-sins section, I reflected on other times I had confessed to God that I was not a good enough wife and I was sorry for not paying more attention to my husband. I would ask God to help me in that area. I have always said one should be careful what one prays for. God answered my prayers and tested me at the same time. I have learned to pay attention to my husband, and I have also learned to love him even more than I thought possible.

We always seem to feel alone in times of sadness or fear. However, we don't have to stay that way. When I was a little girl and felt sad, my mother used to recite the beginning of a poem. She would say, "Laugh, and the world laughs with you. Cry, and you cry alone. The poem is called "Solitude," and it was written by Ella Wheeler Wilcox between 1825 and 1919. I would like to share a couple of stanzas with you.

> Laugh, and the world laughs with you;
> Weep and you weep alone.
> For the sad old earth
> Must borrow its mirth,
> But has trouble enough of its own.

> Sing, and the hills will answer;
> Sigh, it is lost on the air.
> The echoes bound to a joyful sound,
> But shrink from voicing care.

I have learned that my life is not a cappella; I am not completely alone. Because of the faith that I have in Jesus, I am assured that He is with me always.

My song of praise: "The Strength of the Lord" by Larnelle Harris. Bible quote: (Matthew 28:20 NAS) "I am with you always, even to the end of the age."

CHAPTER 15

Finale: Just Say, "Thank You," and Take a Bow

In music, the term *finale* is the last and, as a rule, liveliest movement of a multi-movement instrumental work, or the culminating section of an operatic act or scene usually involving a vocal ensemble rather than a single singer. All in all, it suggests the end. We all approach the finale of our lives. It's a time when we review our past and most often wonder if the directions and decisions we've made were correct. Of course, we all have regrets and remember choices that led to hurt and pain. We must also remember the good choices that led to success. All the good with the bad is part of life. I am at the end of my life. It's a time when all the accumulation of my experiences and knowledge can be used.

Let's consider the end. There are many. I would like to invite you to think about the following ends: the end to a story presented on TV, on a written page, or a song with the last note being held to the extent, or the end of one's breath. The end of a toilet paper roll can be uncomfortable in some cases. There is the end of my bed, where the cat sleeps once in a while. The end to a marriage—how sad is that? How about sitting as a child on the end of a dock and dangling feet over the edge while watching the sun set, signaling the end to another day? I've seen the back end of a cow, a truck, a wagon, a house, and a tractor. How about the front end of a car? Does that even make sense? There's nothing like the end to a good movie or the much-appreciated end to a bad one. Upon noticing a woman bending over to weed a garden, I've heard my father-in-law exclaim, "Now there's the back end of a war horse heading east!" There is the end of a meeting, the end of a job, the end to a life. "Don't touch the end of a match. It will burn." Dessert follows the end of a meal. Some streets are dead ends. And there's that old favorite of women everywhere regarding their hair: the split end. Football has a tight end, not to be confused with the end zone. Many contracts have loose ends. I like the end of a loaf of bread or the crust. Mostly, I like it slathered with butter. What is the end to end all ends?

End—it's just a three-letter word, but very powerful in its usage. So what would I like to end? I would end world hunger, wars, fighting, disease ... I would end anti-Christian behavior, anti-anything behavior, including greed in politicians and power that corrupts those in power.

Finale does not have to be the end; sometimes, it's the beginning. We need to trust in God to know the difference. When I think of my beginning, I remember music being present. The first song I ever heard, or at least remember, was played on an old Victor Victrola record player that sat in my mother's living room. She would turn the handle to wind it up, place the yellow record in the top, set the needle down, and out would come music. I thought the song was wonderful. It started out with this: *"A frog he would a-wooing go, heigh ho!' says Rowley."* Eventually, I learned to turn the handle and play the record over and over. My poor mother! Music was important to me even at the age of five.

During my life, I have listened to and presented more songs than I can count. The Christian songs are my favorite because the words are healing when broken hearts need mending or joyful in times of celebration. Words and melodies mix to give peace and comfort to a tired soul and reminders of days spent in church.

No life is perfect, and no dream is realized exactly as it was imagined. Unless we accept the unwelcome parts of our lives instead of resenting them, we can't completely enjoy all the good things that come our way. My dream of singing with a huge choir in California was never realized. Because that was more than twenty years ago, I understand now where God was leading me. I gained valuable knowledge of music while singing in the retirement centers and nursing homes. I've learned that whenever God intervenes in a person's life, that life is changed. Hearing God is not something that comes natural to people, and I think God knows that. He was very gentle with me in allowing me to think that everything I did was my idea. I prayed but never waited around for an answer. God turned my direction without my realization. What I pursued for my own gain, God turned into blessings for people unable to do for themselves. For me, I received joy beyond measure.

Much has happened to me in the last few years. Moving from California to a new home and a new job was stressful. The job I secured was difficult, lasting only a few years, but just long enough to settle some debts. I decided to retire and do some serious writing. My husband and I settled in and went to church in the little town of Glendale. My initial response to going to this Presbyterian church was less than positive. Because my husband chose this church, I was not going to oppose him. I was used to going to a very large church and singing in an eighty-member choir, so you can imagine the culture shock I felt when I sat in the pew and listened to twelve people singing.

What kept me going back to this church were the people who honestly loved and accepted us. The Sunday mornings we spent in church felt like weekly family reunions. When we met with the pastor because we wanted to join the church, I explained my desire to sing.

He told me I could sing whenever I wanted. At that very moment, my attitude started to change. Perhaps this would be a good move after all. I joined the choir; it felt good to sing with a group once again. It amazes me to be a part of God's direction for my life. At least now in my older years, I have learned to recognize his prompting.

The church service was different from the church I attended in Modesto, California. There were parts I liked and parts I thought unnecessary. The unnecessary part was the children's time. Approximately ten minutes were devoted to presenting information to several young girls and boys who would sit on a bench by the altar. Mrs. Smith (not her real name) would preach, give out a small gift, and send them downstairs for Sunday school. I thought it was a waste of time, mostly because I couldn't hear what she was saying. I even suggested to the pastor to get rid of it. I told him that the children could go straight to Sunday school. After a while, I just ignored that part of the service.

When Mrs. Smith announced that she would be moving out of the area, I thought, *Good, we won't have to listen to ten minutes of children's lessons.* After church that same day, the pastor asked if I would be willing to take over the children's time after Mrs. Smith left. I responded with, "Are you kidding? Just eliminate it. I don't want to do it." He persisted, saying, "Would you please pray about it?" Well, I knew that I was not going to do it, but I thought perhaps I could find someone who would. During a three-week period, I asked at least four people if they were interested. Each person responded, "Thank you, but no, thank you." That settled it for me; they should just eliminate that part of the service.

Finally, the Sunday arrived when Mrs. Smith was gone. After the choir sang and the fellowship part of the service was over, "the sit-down group," as they are called, finished their song. I looked up to see what would come next, and there they were, six children sitting on the bench behind the altar and waiting for children's time. I just couldn't let them sit there alone, so after being prompted by the Holy Spirit, I walked to the front of the church and gave them a word. My presentation took less than five minutes, and I had no gift. Did I mention how nervous I felt?

After church, I was eye-to-eye with the pastor, and again, his question came with a please. I prayed about it and decided that someone had to do it, so why not me? After three days, I called the pastor and told him I would do it, but there would be no gifts. I received many compliments from the congregation. I guess I didn't realize that they too would benefit from my word of the week. Eighteen months have passed, and I am still doing this task that I originally thought should be eliminated. God did not agree with me and again prompted me to step out of my comfort zone.

It would seem that God wasn't done with me, even though I thought I was retired. The year 2013 started out badly for me and also for my church. I've told you about my husband's stroke and how I dealt with it. The church suffered a loss when the choir director and piano player left. There was no choir and no piano during the service. I wasn't too affected, because I missed a lot of church taking care of my husband as he recovered from his stroke. The pastor was concerned with a pre-Easter service called Maundy Thursday. He needed a program and a choir director. My first thought was, *Oh no, not again.* I couldn't do that job. However, after sixty-odd years, I have learned to be open-minded when it comes to church problems.

It seems after I declined the offer to lead the choir, another gal volunteered. The only thing I had to do was come up with a program. I knew I could do that. I sure had enough music at home to access. I prayed about it and put together a program with about five songs and dialogue. Maundy Thursday is the portrayal of the crucifixion of Christ.

After two weeks, the gal who volunteered decided she could not direct the choir. Again, I stood in front of the pastor while thinking,

Why me? I have a great deal of courage and knew that this was an important program that the church congregation looked forward to each year. I agreed to direct the choir. With not quite three months of practice at once a week, the evening arrived.

I took my place at the music stand and faced the choir. Standing in the choir area were twelve people staring at me and waiting to begin. The pastor's wife was poised at the piano. I felt the eyes of the audience on my back, waiting in anticipation to hear the program. A little voice inside my head kept saying, "You're not a choir director. You're not a choir director." I lifted my hands to begin the song, and at that moment, peace entered my heart. I knew that all things are possible with God. I lowered my hands, and the beautiful voices responded. *Here we go*, I thought, *another scared-to-death moment that God has prepared for me.*

I have read many times that God never gives more than a person can handle. As proof, we got through Maundy Thursday successfully. I even directed the choir in a couple of Sunday services. Now I am considered the choir director, and I look forward to September when the choir starts practicing for church. So with much trepidation, forward I go. My schooling in music spanned a twenty-year period performing in nursing homes and retirement centers. I never thought that I would be doing what I'm doing in a little church in a small town in the woods of Oregon. However, God knew.

There are many things I most likely will never do again. I won't be getting up at 5:00 a.m. to participate in a golf tournament, as I did at a young age. I won't be chasing cows through a pasture in an effort to get them into a barn. I won't be having any more babies or starting any children in first grade. However, that's okay. I've lived a lot of good years. I'm prepared for whatever direction God chooses for me. I've finally learned to listen. I've learned to sing my song and when I'm finished to take a bow and say, "Thank you."

I have a deep love for music and a fanatical need to share it to whomever will listen. I find a song, study the words and the message, listen to the tone of the notes, and feel how the song is affecting me. I practice until I am ready to share. I sing of God's love and mercy. I sing of His gift of salvation through belief in His son, Jesus. It is *Of Thee I Sing.*

Another Sunday morning is here and I'm standing in front of the congregation at this wonderful community church. I am ready. Just before I pick up the microphone, my heart is thumping and I struggle to organize the butterflies in my stomach. My mind touches briefly on the love I have for Christ, and I feel His peace as I search for that first note.

Let the music begin!

My song of praise: "I Will Call upon the Lord" by Michael O'Shields. Bible quote: (Exodus 15:2 NAS) "The Lord is my strength and song and He has become my salvation."

I play

Of Thee I Sing, "Hallelujah"
A song by Dianne Coon

There's a church in the valley, where we all go on Sunday,
Singing, "Glory! Hallelujah! Praise the Lord!"
This church is filled with people, hugging on each other.
With words of love exchanged and thoughts of one accord.

Of Thee I sing, "Hallelujah!" God's love will travel through ya.
At this church in the valley, where we'll all go to pray.

We all sit together and pray for one another.
There're joys and concerns with blessings all around.
So come on in and join us, lift your voice and sing.
Raise your hands in worship to Jesus Christ, the King.

Mary's by the front door, greetin' everyone,
A big ole smile upon her face.
The pastor starts a-praying, And the candle needs a light,
The choir starts singing Amazing Grace, "Amazing Grace!"

This little church in Glendale is busting at the seams,
With people singing songs of love and grace.
We all love the Father with one thought in mind:
To make this world a better place.

Of Thee I sing, "Hallelujah!"
God's love will travel through ya.
At this church in the valley, where we'll all go to pray.

Of Thee I sing, "Hallelujah!"
God's love will travel through ya.
At this church in the valley, where we'll all go to pray.

References

Alabama, Canadian Singing Group. 1970s.

Author unknown. "A Frog He Would a Wooing Go."

Author unknown. "Just a Closer Walk with Thee."

Author unknown. "The Loom of Time" (poem).

Boerksen, Brian. "Come Now Is the Time to Worship."

Boston Philharmonic Orchestra. American Orchestra. Founded 1881.

Carnegie, Dale. *How to Win Friends & Influence People.*

Carnegie, Dale. "Principles of Human Behavior."

Carter, R. Kelso. "Standing on the Promises."

Coon, Dianne. "Of Thee I Sing, Hallelujah."

Crouch, Andrae. "Through It All."

Dacre, Harry. "A Bicycle Built for Two."

Davidson, Robert. "The Steadfast Love of the Lord Never Ceases."

Denver, John, et al. "Take Me Home, Country Roads."

Espinosa, Eddie. "Change My Heart, Oh God."

Ferguson, Greg. "He Is Able."

Graham, David. "In Moments Like These."

Grimm, Jacob, and Wilhelm Grimm. "Snow White and the Seven Dwarfs."

Gruber, Xaver, and Joseph Mohr. "Silent Night."

Harris, Larnelle. "The Strength of the Lord."

Hudson, Bob. "Humble Thyself in the Sight of the Lord."

Kilpatrick, Bob. "In My Life, Lord, Be Glorified."

Klein, Laurie. "I Love You, Lord."

Lehman, Ernest. "Climb Every Mountain."

Lendeman, Edith, and Carl Statz. "Little Things Mean a Lot."

Martin, Civilla D., and Charles H. Gabriel. "His Eye Is on the Sparrow."

Miles, Charles Austin. "In the Garden."

O'Shields, Michael. "I Will Call upon The Lord."

Patty, Sandy. "In the Garden Medley."

Rodgers, Richard, and Oscar Hammerstein. "The Sound of Music."

Schuler, George, and Ira Wilson. "Make Me a Blessing."

Scriven, Joseph M. "What a Friend We Have in Jesus."

Sousa, John Philip. "The Washington Post March."

Stewart, Redd and Pee Wee King. "Tennessee Waltz."

Styne, et al. "Doe a Deer."

The Moody Bible Institute. The Ryrie Study Bible. New American Standard Translation.

Vejvoda, Jaromir. "Beer Barrel Polka."

Walker, Jerry Jeff. "Mr. Bojangles."

Ward, Jay, and Alex Anderson. "Rocky the Flying Squirrel."

Webster's Standard Dictionary. Trident Reference Publishing. 2006 edition.

Weiss, Stephan, and Bernie Baum. "Music, Music, Music."

Wilcox, Ella Wheeler. "Solitude" (poem).

Wilkin, Marijohn, and Kris Kristofferson. "One Day at a Time."